WESTMAR COLLEGE

P9-DOF-617

Synchronistic events can assure us when we are on the right life-path and advise us when we are not; at the most profound level, they reassure us that we are not mere observers, but "always participators in an interconnected cosmic web."

Photo by James Bolen

Jean Shinoda Bolen, M.D., is a psychiatrist and Jungian analyst, an Associate Clinical Professor of Psychiatry at the University of California Medical Center in San Francisco, Fellow of the American Psychiatric Association, Vice-Chairperson of the Council of National Affairs of the A.P.A., a Diplomate of the American Board of Psychiatry and Neurology, Member of the International Association for Analytic Psychology and the Society of Jungian Analysts of Northern California.

Dr. Bolen is married to James Bolen, Editor and President of *New Realities* magazine, for which she is Editorial Advisor. The Bolens have two children and live in Mill Valley, California.

The Tao of Psychology

Jean Shinoda Bolen, M.D.

THE TAO OF PSYCHOLOGY

Synchronicity and the Self

Published in San Francisco by
HARPER & ROW, PUBLISHERS
New York Hagerstown San Francisco London

BF
698
.B582

THE TAO OF PSYCHOLOGY: Synchronicity and the Self.
Copyright © 1979 by Jean Shinoda Bolen. All rights re-
served. Printed in the United States of America. No part of
this book may be used or reproduced in any manner whatso-
ever without written permission except in the case of brief
quotations embodied in critical articles and reviews. For information address Harper & Row, Publishers, Inc., 10 East
53rd Street, New York, NY 10022. Published simultaneously
in Canada by Fitzhenry & Whiteside, Limited, Toronto.

Designed by Paul Quin

Library of Congress Cataloging in Publication Data

Bolen, Jean Shinoda.
  The Tao of psychology.

  Bibliography: p. 104
  Includes index.
  1. Personality. 2. Self. 3. Coincidence.
4. Tao. 5. Jung, Carl Gustav, 1875–1961. I. Title.
BF698.B582   150'.19'54   79–1778
ISBN 0–06–250080–5

  80 81 82 83 10 9 8 7 6 5 4 3 2

98373

Except for the point, the still point,
There would be no dance, and there is only the dance.
                                              T. S. Eliot

To Jim, Melody, and Andy—
as we dance around the still point

Contents

ACKNOWLEDGMENTS

Excerpts reprinted by permission from:

I Ching or *Book of Changes,* rendered into English by Cary F. Baynes, Bollingen Series XIX. Copyright 1950, © 1967 by Princeton University Press. Copyright © renewed 1977 by Princeton University Press.

The Collected Works of C. G. Jung, translated by R. F. C. Hull, Bollingen Series XX. Volume 8: "The Structure and Dynamics of the Psyche" copyright © 1960 by Princeton University Press. Volume 9,1: "The Archetypes of the Collective Unconcious" copyright © 1959, 1969 by Princeton University Press. Volume 14: "Mysterium Coniunctionis" copyright © 1963 by Princeton University Press. Volume 15: "The Spirit in Man, Art, and Literature," copyright © 1966 by Princeton University Press. Volume 16: "The Practice of Psychotherapy" copyright © 1954, 1966 by Princeton University Press.

Four Quartets by T. S. Eliot, copyright 1943 by T. S. Eliot; copyright 1971 by Esme Valerie Eliot. Reprinted with permission of Harcourt, Brace, Jovanovich, Inc.

Tao Te Ching by Lao-Tzu, copyright © 1972 by Gia-fu Feng and Jane English. Reprinted by permission of Alfred A. Knopf, Inc.

Memories, Dreams and Reflections by *C. G. Jung,* recorded and edited by Aniela Jaffé, translated from the German by Richard and Clara Winston. Translational copyright © 1962, 1963, by Random House, Inc. Reprinted by permission of Pantheon Books, a division of Random House, Inc.

Illusions: The Adventures of a Reluctant Messiah by Richard Bach. Copyright © 1977 by Creature Enterprises, Inc. Reprinted by permission of Delacorte Press/Eleanor Friede.

Preface

"When the pupil is ready, the teacher will come." This ancient Chinese saying describes an idea basic to Eastern thought: the connection between the human psyche and external events, between inner and outer world. Synchronicity, defined by C. G. Jung as "meaningful coincidence," is one way in which this connection is expressed in our daily lives. The Eastern mind has considered the underlying connection between ourselves and others, between ourselves and the universe, the essential reality and called it the Tao. For those who have felt the power of events, dreams, and meetings that seem to contain meanings deeper than themselves, it can be a window on a world larger and more whole than the world of logical reasoning and concrete facts.

Because interconnectedness and totality are my subjects, the structure of this book is not linear. Instead, this will be a circular journey around the subject—or to use Jung's jaw-breaking word, a "circumambulation," revealing aspects that can be focused on, illuminating a part at a time—much as the Pioneer probe of Venus circled the planet, taking a series of photographs. The chapters are like these photographs, each one showing an aspect of synchronicity and the Tao from a different perspective.

My own introduction to the Tao was through personal experience. Explanations followed later. For those who find most meaning in ideas, I present the explanations that evolved from my experience—the concept that synchronicity is equivalent to the Tao, and the reasons why we Westerners have had trouble appreciating this Eastern concept of underlying reality. Others may find themselves reliving a memory of having had a Tao experience—through which the idea can be intuitively known.

My understanding of Jung's concepts of synchronicity, the archetypes of the collective unconscious, and the Self developed along with my career in psychiatry. An understanding of Jungian theory is helpful in grasping the full meaning of synchronicity; however, understanding can also come through the examples and descriptions on which the middle chapters focus.

Synchronicity can be most immediately appreciated when we see how it operates in our everyday lives. I would like to share with you the methods I have developed to notice and delve into the possible meaning of a synchronistic event and to understand how each synchronistic event can connect us to something specific in ourselves, as well as revealing connections with others.

In addition to explaining daily events, the concept of synchronicity can give us new insight into certain ideas. The *I Ching,* for instance, is an oracular method in which a questioner deliberately produces a "reading" through synchronicity, which then counsels actions or attitudes appropriate to the time and situation. Synchronicity sheds light on research into parapsychology, which substantiates the existence of connections between ourselves and others or objects.

Much of the value of synchronicity lies in its ability to connect us to a meaning-giving, intuitively known principle in our lives by which we can find a "path with heart," a *tao,* a way to live in harmony with the universe. Synchronicity can provide us with confirmation that we are on the right path, as well as let us know when we are not.

Finally, at the most profound level, synchronicity can lead us to the awareness that we are part of something far greater than ourselves, and to a sense of wholeness in the archetype of the Self, metaphorically expressed by the Grail Legend, by the concept of the Kingdom of God, or by returning to the Tao.

Thank You

For sharing a synchronistic event, for editorial advice, for helpful information, for typing, for having had something to do with helping this book happen: David F. Brown, Lois Bullis, Marie Cantlon, Georgiana Cummings, Tenita Deal, Mary Ivy Dekker, Kathleen Gauen, James Goodwin, Jean Hayes, Kay Hensley, Ann Hogle, Nancy Haugen, Chauncey Irvine, Donna Kasper, David Lombardi, Jr., Irene Peck, Linda Purrington, Sarah Rush, Cornelia Schulz, Nancy Scotton, Frederick Steele, Lynn Thomas, Judy Vibberts, Kimberley Wilkins, Carol Wolman, Jim Yandell.

Although I'm the author of this book, I feel I've also been a privileged participant in a synchronistic happening. From the very beginning, happy coincidences have played a part, as people and events have cooperated, facilitated, and supported its creation and publication. I also trust that this book will reach whomever it was meant to—synchronistically— and get wherever it is supposed to go.

Jean Bolen
Mill Valley, California
March 1979

The Tao that can be told is not the eternal Tao.
The name that can be named is not the eternal name.
The nameless is the beginning of heaven and earth.
The named is the mother of ten thousand things.
Ever desireless, one can see the mystery.
Ever desiring, one can see the manifestations.
These two spring from the same source but differ in
    name; this appears as darkness.
Darkness within darkness.
The gate to all mystery.

Lao Tsu, *Tao Te Ching*
Translated by Gia-Fu Feng
and Jane English

CHAPTER 1

WHAT THE TAO IS— WHAT THE DANCE IS

A personal perspective on understanding the Tao of Eastern religion · How synchronicity is the only psychological equivalent to the Tao Why we Westerners have so much trouble with the concept—it's the way our minds work

I went to the mountains when I was a youngster and lay in my sleeping bag under the stars, seeing the vastness of the Milky Way above. What my eyes saw, my soul experienced. I felt a sense of reverence and awe at the boundlessness and beauty of the universe. It touched me. I felt God's presence in the mountains, trees, and immense sky. What was above me and around me and included me was unlimited, eternal, and alive. It moved me. Wisps of clouds would pass overhead. I would see a shooting star and make a wish, and, without knowing when, seeing would end and sleep would begin. It comforted me. Then morning would come, crisp and invigorating, and I would awaken to find the sky blue or gray or brilliantly dawning in gold and orange. Not a star would be seen in the now bright sky. It would be time to get up and get moving, to be up and about.

Most of the time, we are all up and about, coping with what needs to be done and with the people around us. We focus on what is in front of us, dealing with the tangibles of our lives in the hurried time and limited space available. In the light of our everyday world, we cannot see the stars. Even at night, our vision of the heavens is limited by the lights of our cities and the pollution in the air from our machines. We are enclosed in buildings, walled in, nature around us shut out; we are kept too busy with the events of our evenings to be able to look up and experience the awesomeness of the nighttime sky. But whether seen or unseen, the stars are there. There is an expanding, infinite, timeless, yet moving universe of which we are a part. To know this intuitively, by glimpsing a portion of the heavens at night before falling asleep once again, can be similar to what the Zen student seeks in meditation—that moment of sudden enlightenment in which the *vision of the Tao* is experienced.

Whether I am lying under the stars or sitting in Zazen meditating, or at peace in prayer, the *intuitive* knowledge that there is a patterned universe, or an underlying *meaning* to all experience, or a primal source, *to which "I" am connected,* always evokes a feeling of reverence. It is something known rather than thought about, so that explanatory words are inadequate; as the *Tao Te Ching,* by Lao Tsu, begins, *"The Tao that can be told is not the eternal Tao."* Yet examples help in the understanding—because almost all of us, often early in our lives, have had an intimation of what is called the *Tao.*

Frederick Franck, artist and author of *The Zen of Seeing: Seeing/ Drawing as Meditation,* wrote about a moment of intuitive insight into this reality, which he experienced from an introverted perspective (as mine under the stars was an extrovert's perception of participation in something that seemed "out there," yet included me).

On a dark afternoon—I was ten or eleven—I was walking on a country road. On my left a patch of curly kale, on my right some yellowed Brussels sprouts. I felt a snowflake on my cheek, and from far away in the charcoal-gray sky, I saw the slow approach of a snow storm. I stood still.

Some flakes were now falling around my feet. A few melted as they hit the ground. Others stayed intact. Then I heard the falling of the snow, with the softest hissing sound.

I stood transfixed, listening . . . and knew what can never be expressed: that the natural is supernatural, and that I am the eye that hears and the ear that sees. And what is outside happens in me, that outside and inside are unseparated.

Although words cannot express fully or adequately describe the essence of something experienced intuitively such as the eternal Tao, or the reality of God, because it has a quality of revelation, words can transmit the idea. There are good reasons to discuss that which cannot be known fully through words—because the way for an experience to happen can be prepared. Intellectual awareness and acceptance of a spiritual concept, coupled with receptivity or openness, lay the groundwork for an intuitively felt experience that can then follow. As the Eastern saying goes, "*When the pupil is ready, the teacher will come.*"

The eternal Tao or great Tao had many names representing the idea that there is an eternal law or principle at work, underlying what appeared as a perpetually changing world in motion. Taoists referred to it by many names, including the Primal Unity and Source, the Cosmic Mother, the Infinite and Ineffable Principle of Life, the One. Tao has been referred to as the right, the moral order, the principle, the nature of life forces, the idea of the world, the method, or the way. Some even have translated it as God. Richard Wilhelm, the sinologist and translator of the *I Ching* translated *Tao* as "meaning." In many respects, the concept of Tao resembles the Greek concept of logos. In modern translations of the New Testament into Chinese, *logos* is translated as *Tao;* the Gospel of St. John then opens, "*In the beginning was the Tao.*"

All efforts to explain the Tao use words that stand for abstract ideas or metaphors. The *Tao Te Ching* says,

> The Tao is an empty vessel, it is used but never filled . . .
> hidden deep but ever present . . . like water which gives life to
> the ten thousand things but does not strive . . . it cannot be seen
> —it is beyond form, it cannot be heard—it is beyond sound, it
> cannot be held—it is intangible . . . it cannot be exhausted
> . . . the Tao is hidden and without name, the Tao alone
> nourishes and brings everything to fulfillment . . . all things arise
> from the Tao . . . it is the source of the ten thousand things
> . . . the great Tao flows everywhere.

The experience of the Tao or of a unifying principle in the universe to which everything in the world relates, underlies the major Eastern religions—Hinduism, Buddhism, Confucianism, Taoism, and Zen. Although each religion may call the experience by a different name, the essence of all varieties of Eastern mysticism is the same. Each holds that all phenomena—people, animals, plants, and objects from atomic particles to galaxies are aspects of the One.

In the *Bhagavad Gita,* the most well-known religious poem of Hinduism, the god Krishna's spiritual instruction is based on the concept that all the myriad of things and profusion of events around us are manifestations of the same ultimate reality, called *Brahman*—the inner essence of all things; its qualities are as the *Tao*—beginningless, incomprehensible, indescribable, an ever-transforming essence of all things, unifying and underlying the numerous gods and goddesses that are worshipped. The manifestation of Brahman in the human soul is *Atman;* Atman an aspect of the one cosmic reality of Brahman.

Buddhism speaks of attaining through a mystical experience of awakening, the reality of *acintya* where all elements are as one, undivided "suchness" or *tathata,* participating in the all-pervading Buddha essense of *Dharmakaya.* Zen emphasizes the experience of enlightenment or *satori,* the direct mystical awareness of the Buddha nature of all things, where one experiences being an integral part of the great continuum of all that is. Confucianism and Taoism are two complementary poles, one pragmatic, the other mystical; underlying both—the concept of the eternal Tao.

While the major Eastern religions are based on the perception of the unity and interrelationship of all things and events, and experience the many forms of the ten thousand things as manifestations of a basic oneness, the orthodox Judeo-Christian tradition emphasizes opposing dualities: God above, sinful human below, soul in opposition to world, spirit struggling to overcome flesh, upright man resisting Eve-like woman.

Until recently the concept of Eastern totality has been absent from Western scientific thinking, which focuses on duplicatable experiments based on cause and effect, in which one distinct variable at a time could be considered. Any "oneness" between observer and the observed was "unthinkable," as in "too ridiculous" rather than as in "wisdom beyond thought." But with the advent of quantum physics and relativity theory, a radical transformation is taking place.

Fritjof Capra, in *The Tao of Physics,* postulates that modern atomic physics leads us to a view of reality that is very similar to the Eastern mystic's intuitive vision of reality. The picture of an interconnected cosmic web in which the human observer is always a participator emerges from quantum physics. At the atomic particle level, the world view becomes very Eastern and mystical; time and space become a continuum, matter and energy interchange, observer and observed interact.

It fascinates me to realize that the "answers" to the question about the nature of the universe at which Western science is arriving through sophisticated, extraordinarily expensive, sensitive machinery, and complex, hardly comprehensible mathematical formulas is, on the face of it, the same as what an Eastern mystic in solitary meditation knows as the eternal Tao. Both share two basic themes: the unity and interrelationship of all phenomena and the intrinsically dynamic nature of the universe.

Western philosophy, like Western religion, has been dominated by the spirit-matter duality. Réne Descartes' "Cartesian" division of nature into two fundamentally different worlds, of mind and of matter, is a prime example of what has held sway, paralleled by classical "Newtonian" physics, with its mechanistic model of the universe. Just as there have been Western mystics in the closets of orthodoxy, there have been philosophers who envisioned a continuously changing, inter-related universe. Two of the most noteworthy come to mind: Heraclitus of Ephesus, who taught that everything grows and is eternally in the process of becoming, and Gottfried Wilhelm von Leibniz, who saw the human as a microcosmic expression of the macrocosm.

In psychology, only C. G. Jung has addressed this issue, describing synchronistic events as manifestations of the acausal connecting principle that is equivalent to the Tao. He theorized that people as well as all animate and inanimate objects are linked through a collective unconscious. Just as modern atomic physics acknowledges that the researcher affects whatever he or she studies at the particle level, Jung suggested that the psyche of the observing person interacts in the moment with the events of the outside world.

Jung described synchronicity as an acausal connecting principle that manifests itself through meaningful coincidences. There are no rational explanations for these situations in which a person has a thought, dream, or inner psychological state that coincides with an event. For example, a woman has a vivid dream that her sister's house is on fire and impulsively calls to see if she is all right—there is a fire, and the call that awakened her may have saved her life. Or, a researcher is stumped at a crucial point needing some obscure highly technical information, and at a fund-raising dinner finds himself unexpectedly seated next to a person who has the information. A woman arrives in a city, wanting to contact a former roommate, cannot locate her, and steps into a crowded elevator to find she is standing there. I think of someone, the phone rings, and the caller is the person whom I've had on my mind.

All these are examples of synchronicity, varying from the dramatic to the commonplace. In each situation, a person was struck by the coincidence and could not explain how it could have come about. Intuitively, each event felt significant and raised the possibility of there being an invisible, unknown connection or way in which such things happen.

Jung, by saying this phenomenon was "synchronicity," gave it a name. He also indicated its importance, saying that, *"The understanding of synchronicity is the key which unlocks the door to the Eastern apperception of totality that we find so mysterious."*

Through synchronicity the Western mind may come to know what the Tao is. As a concept, synchronicity bridges East and West, philosophy and psychology, right brain and left. Synchronicity is the Tao of psychology, relating the individual to the totality. If we personally realize that synchronicity is at work in our lives, we feel connected, rather than isolated and estranged from others; we feel ourselves part of a divine, dynamic, interrelated universe. Synchronistic events offer us perceptions that may be useful in our psychological and spiritual growth and may reveal to us, through intuitive knowledge, that our lives have meaning.

Every time I have become aware of a synchronistic experience, I have had an accompanying feeling that some grace came along with it. Each time another person has shared a synchronistic event with me, I felt like a privileged participant. There is something awesome and humbling, yet moving and knowing about glimpsing the Tao through synchronistic events.

Just as stars cannot be seen in midday, yet are there nonetheless, in our Western minds the conditions are not right for "seeing" a pattern of underlying oneness. Recent interest in right and left cerebral hemisphere brain functioning may explain why the conditions for perception are not right. We have favored a certain kind of consciousness at the expense of another. Research into how our brains work shows that it is correct to sometimes say, "I have two minds about this," because we do have two minds that function quite differently within our heads. Like night and day, the right and left cerebral hemispheres are different in their perceptions and way of working.

The left hemisphere contains our speech centers, controls the right half of our bodies, and uses the logic and reasoning of linear thinking to arrive at assessments or conclusions. It focuses on what is tangible and measurable; "left brain" thinking is the basis for all scientific experimentation and observation. The left hemisphere sees the "bits" or "parts" and the cause-and-effect relationships between them, rather than the whole interacting picture. Its relationship to the world is to see the world as being separate from itself, something to use or to dominate—its style is active and "masculine."

The right cerebral hemisphere is quite different: Images, rather than words, are its tools. It knows through intuition what the totality of a picture is, and also experiences a sense of what something emerged from and what it may become. The "right brain" can contain ambiguities and opposites. It takes in the whole of an event at once, rather than focusing on a detail or part, and can simultaneously perceive and feel about what it takes in. The right hemisphere compares through metaphor rather than measurement. Its style is receptive and reflective, a more "feminine" mode than that of the left hemisphere.

The masculine culture of the Western world has devalued right hemisphere functioning, and our experience collectively and individually is poorer for that devaluation. Intuition is put down as mere "woman's intuition"; reacting to a situation on a feeling level is drummed out of little boys, who are urged to be logical at all times. The message of our culture is that artists, musicians, poets, and women can function through these "inferior" ways, but real men do not. Consequently, anything that cannot be perceived and judged through the five senses and thinking is considered of little value, and gradually many individuals cease to experience what it is like to be moved emotionally by music, or by a symbol, or to have an intuition about an underlying reality.

Western civilization has thus allowed one-half of the brain to devalue, repress, and dominate the intuitive perceptions of the other. For it is through intuition that we can experience the totality and underlying connections or patterns invisible to the senses, that have been so central to Eastern thought. We need not travel to the East to become aware of its wisdom; rather, since we have the potential within us to perceive, and need only awaken it, the journey to the East is really an inward one.

As valuable as the intellect is, it has limitations related to the question of "whole and part"; R. H. Blyth, the haiku scholar, described it thus, *"The intellect can understand any part of a thing as a part, but not as a whole. It can understand anything which God is not."* To experience the eternal Tao requires that our consciousness perceive through the workings of the right cerebral hemisphere, turning off the analytical, skeptical workings of the left hemisphere. As Goethe observed, we murder when we dissect. We kill off the vitality of the experience, murder the spirit, and deny the soul, when we require that everything be processed through our left hemisphere's logical computerlike workings.

By our insistence that the scientific method is the only means by which anything can be known, doors of perception are closed, the wisdom of the East is denied us, and our own inner world becomes one-sided. East and West are two halves of a whole; they represent the two inner aspects of each individual man and woman. The psychological split needs healing through an inner union, allowing flow between left and right hemispheres, between scientific and spiritual, masculine and feminine, yin and yang.

When we, with our Western-focused consciousness, also become able to perceive spiritual reality, it is then possible for us to be aware of being separate individuals and also conscious of relating to a greater whole; of living in a world of linear time, yet capable of experiencing the timelessness of an eternal reality of which we are a part; of seeing with daylight perception as well as starlight vision. Our consciousness is then experienced as moving, rather than fixed.

T. S. Eliot explores this interplay in his *Four Quartets.* In one of these poems, *Burnt Norton,* a passage specifically conveys this relationship between a "still point" and the "dance" that is like the *Tao* underlying all movement or like the stillness of God at the heart of all activity.

At the still point of the turning world. Neither flesh nor fleshless;
Neither from nor towards: at the still point, there the dance is,

But neither arrest nor movement. And do not call it fixity,
Where past and future are gathered. Neither movement from
   nor towards,
Neither ascent nor decline. Except for the point, the still point,
There would be no dance, and there is only the dance.

To continue with Eliot's metaphor, we are part of a dance in which nothing that happens to us or in us ever repeats itself exactly, while the underlying connecting principle to which everything in the universe relates, including us, remains always the same.

CHAPTER 2

JUNG, SYNCHRONICITY, AND THE SELF

A personal journey into psychiatry and Jungian analytic training · An introduction to Jung's concepts of archetypes, the collective unconscious, synchronicity, and the Self

T hrough a series of encounters and events, I became a Jungian analyst. I did not start out to be one, however. In my last year at medical school, I thought about becoming a psychiatrist because the experience of seeing patients in the adult psychiatry clinic and the outpatient department in my junior and senior years had been interesting and rewarding. Talking with me, as unexperienced as I was, had seemed helpful to them. So I applied to the Langley Porter Neuropsychiatric Institute, which is part of the University of California Medical Center in San Francisco, where I was a medical student. Then, thinking better of it, I failed to follow through by seeking letters of recommendation. Instead, leaning toward internal medicine, I began a rotating internship at Los Angeles County Hospital, opting for medicine as my first rotation. I had been at the county hospital long enough to miss San Francisco and had acquired quite a bit of experience treating the medical complications of alcoholism—cirrhotic livers, bleeding esophageal varices, gastritis, incipient delirium tremens, and the like—when, totally unexpectedly, I received a wire from Langley Porter saying they had accepted me into their residency program.

They must have used my medical student evaluations in lieu of letters of recommendation. I was requested to notify them of my answer by return wire. The requirement for a quick decision led to my impulsive acceptance, influenced primarily by the opportunity to return to San Francisco, which I missed. I still was not sure I wanted to be a psychiatrist, but I rationalized that I at least could begin the residency. If it turned out that psychiatry wasn't for me, the year's experience would be helpful in whatever else I might do.

I began my residency on an inpatient service, where people were hospitalized because they had either become psychotic, out of touch with reality, and temporarily unable to function or were suicidal and needed to be hospitalized to keep them alive during a severe depression. I was assigned responsibility for six patients. They were "first admissions"—individuals who had never been hospitalized before. Rather than being weird or strange to me, I found that they were people who had been managing, until they had become overwhelmed. In every one of them, there was both a healthy ally for me to work with and a sick part that was destructive or hopeless, hallucinated, deluded, or obsessed. I found I could understand their situation and that I cared about them. Rather than treating a disease, I was now treating a whole person, not merely a "case of" something. From my encounter with these six patients, I knew within the first week that, serendipitously, I had found my life work.

Residents are assigned supervisors throughout the three years of training. Most supervisors, like the residency itself, were Freudian or eclectic, although there were a small handful of Jungian psychiatrists for supervisors. In the luck of the draw, John Perry and Donald Sandner were assigned as my supervisors. Joseph Wheelwright meanwhile was holding forth in a Jungian seminar in the basement, while further along I acquired another Jungian, John Talley, for a consultant on a long-term case. Later I realized that Langley Porter is the only university residency in the United States that had Jungian supervisors or seminars and that my particular experience as a resident was very unusual. Except for these seemingly "accidental" encounters, I would have had no exposure to C. G. Jung's ideas.

What I gained from Dr. Wheelwright—a tall, warm, very delightful man whose seminars were informal, not theoretical, and often uproariously funny, since he was a marvelous mimic with a fund of stories—was a sense of Jung. Dr. Wheelwright had been analyzed by Jung and was one of the founders of the C. G. Jung Institute of San Francisco.

The image of Jung that emerged was of a larger-than-life man, a Swiss farm peasant in appearance rather than a scholarly intellectual. I learned he had a charismatic vitality that drew people to him, a belly laugh, and an expressive spontaneity (which certainly doesn't emerge in his writings). The creativity and breadth of his thinking were truly impressive, while his intuition bordered on being psychic, a quality that ran in his family.

I was attracted by Jung's ideas that humans were motivated by creative, reflective and spiritual drives as well as by the aggressive, active, and sexual instincts on which Freud focused. On finishing my residency, I gravitated into the Jungian Institute, not to become an analyst but to learn more. Eight years later, having found that it was indeed the "right" place for me, I did become a certified Jungian analyst.

Somewhere along the way, Dr. Elizabeth Osterman gave a seminar on synchronicity, which was my introduction to the subject. She spoke about synchronicity and the tendency toward patterning in the universe and conveyed a sense that there was something profound and important about the subject that could not be grasped intellectually. At the time, I didn't fully understand what she was talking about, although I intuitively sensed it. Others in the seminar seemed to have even more difficulties. I remember the protestations of one of my colleague-classmates, whose rationality was sorely exercised about this. It seemed that synchronicity was one of Jung's more esoteric theories. Letting the idea go to work in my head, reading more about it over the next few years, and then becoming aware of the synchronistic events that occurred around me, the theoretical concept of synchronicity moved from being an idea to an everyday reality in my life. Now I find it of real value in the practice of psychotherapy as well.

Jung wrote about synchronicity fairly late in his professional life. His major exposition, "Synchronicity: An Acausal Connecting Principle," was published in 1952, when he was in his midseventies. He described it as an effort "to give a consistent account of everything I have to say on the subject," in order to "open up a very obscure field which is philosophically of greatest importance." It is a very complex, multifootnoted elaboration of an essay, "On Synchronicity," that had been given as a lecture the year before. Possibly because this monograph is difficult reading, possibly because the concept itself is difficult to grasp by intellect alone and requires an intuitive facility, synchronicity has been more in the closet than out in the world.

In 1930, Jung had introduced the "synchronistic principle" in a memorial address for his friend, Richard Wilhelm, the sinologist who translated many ancient Chinese texts. His first description of synchronicity however was in the foreword to the Wilhelm-Baynes translation of the *I Ching* or *Book of Changes* in 1949. In the thirty years preceding, Jung had made other fleeting mentions of synchronicity in his lectures and writing. This was a concept long incubated.

"Synchronicity" is a descriptive term for the link between two events that are connected through their meaning, a link that cannot be explained by cause and effect. To illustrate synchronicity, Jung described an incident with a patient, a woman who "always knew better about everything" and whose analysis consequently was not going very well.

After several fruitless attempts to sweeten her rationalism with a somewhat more human understanding, I had to confine myself to the hope that something unexpected and irrational would turn up, something that would burst the intellectual retort into which she had sealed herself. Well, I was sitting opposite her one day with my back to the window, listening to her flow of rhetoric. She had an impressive dream the night before, in which someone had given her a golden scarab—a costly piece of jewelry. While she was still telling me this dream, I heard something behind me gently tapping on the window. I turned around and saw that it was a fairly large flying insect that was knocking against the window-pane from outside in the obvious effort to get into the dark room. This seemed to me very strange. I opened the window immediately and caught the insect in the air as it flew in. It was a scarabaeid beetle, whose gold-green color most nearly resembles that of a golden scarab. I handed the beetle to my patient with the words, "Here is your scarab." This experience punctured the desired hole in her rationalism and broke the ice of her intellectual resistance. The treatment could now be continued with satisfactory results.

For the scarablike beetle to come into the room at that moment was an eerie coincidence for this woman. Meaningful coincidences such as this reach in to touch a deep feeling level in the psyche. This woman needed a transforming emotional experience, which the scarab provided. Interestingly, the event symbolically paralleled her situation. The scarab is an Egyptian symbol of rebirth or transformation—"it" needed to enter the analysis. When the scarabaeid beetle entered the room, transformation of a rigid attitude could begin, new growth could happen.

Synchronicity requires a human participant, for it is a subjective experience in which the person gives meaning to the coincidence. "Meaning" differentiates synchronicity from a synchronous event. A synchronous event is anything simultaneous, events that occur at the same moment. Clocks are synchronized, airplanes are scheduled to take off at the same time, several people walk into the same auditorium at the same moment, but no one sees anything significant in these "coincidences." In synchronicity, however, the meaningful "coincidence" occurs within a subjective time frame. The person links the two events together, and the events need not occur simultaneously, although this is often the case.

Jung described three types of synchronicity. In the first category, there is *a coincidence between mental content (which could be a thought or feeling) and outer event.* This seemed to be the case in an incident between myself and my then four-year-old daughter. I was in the kitchen in the midst of dinner preparation and mentioned to my husband Jim that I needed some flowers for the table. The children were playing outside, quite out of range of hearing. Moments later Melody came in through the length of the house, a bouquet of pink geraniums in her hands, saying "Here, Mommy." The incident of the scarab beetle exemplifies this category, in which the outer event uncannily reflects what is happening psychologically in that moment.

In the second group of synchronistic events, *a person has a dream or vision, which coincides with an event that is taking place at a distance (and is later verified).* It is an awareness of what is happening without using any of the five senses. For example, my grandfather had an uncanny way of knowing when an old friend or relative would die. The person would appear to him in a dream or in a waking vision, carrying a suitcase. In this way, he would know that they were leaving and moving on. My mother remembers his remarking on several occasions that so-and-so died—my grandfather had "seen" him on his way with a suitcase. Then, often weeks later, news would come verifying what Grandfather already knew clairvoyantly. Because he had come to America from Japan, a considerable distance separated my grandfather in New York City from relatives and many old friends. The news took a relatively long time to travel via standard means, by sea over the Pacific, by land to the East Coast. An historical event in this category is Swedenborg's "Vision of the Great Fire" in Stockholm, in which he described what he "saw" to others. Days later, the news arrived of the actual event, which had occurred at the time when he had had the vision and as he had described it.

In the third synchronistic category, *a person has an image (as a dream, vision, or premonition) about something that will happen in the future, which then does occur.* When I was pregnant, my husband Jim was sure about the sex of each child to come, based on a strong psychic impression, and I had the intuition that he really did know. So sure were we that common sense did not prevail—we had only a girl's name, Melody Jean, picked for our first child, our daughter, and only a boy's name for our son, Andre Joseph, who arrived less than two years later. And President Lincoln, just prior to his assassination, reported having dreams in which he saw his body lying in state, which is an historical example of the coincidence between a dream and a future happening.

In each situation, an actual event coincided with a thought, vision, dream, or premonition. My own examples are not particularly dramatic and may not be at all convincing to someone else, yet they stand out in my memory because of the feelings that accompanied the events: the sense of the bond between all of us—that Melody and I were tuned into one another, that Jim would know "who" I was carrying. The accompanying sense of connection is what was meaningful to me when the outer event coincided with the thought or premonition. Synchronicity is the principle that Jung postulates as the link connecting psyche and event in a meaningful coincidence, the participant determining (through purely subjective feelings) whether the coincidences are "meaningful." To *fully* appreciate what a synchronistic event is, one may need to personally experience an uncanny coincidence and feel a spontaneous emotional response—of chills up the spine, or awe, or warmth—feelings that often accompany synchronicity. Ideally, there should be no way to account for the coincidence rationally or by pure chance.

Some important differences exist between synchronicity and causality. Causality has to do with *objective* knowledge: Observation and reasoning are used to explain how one event arises directly out of another. When a rock is thrown at a window and the window breaks, cause and effect are involved. It does not matter who does the throwing, when or where it happens, or who is watching. Causality says that a rock thrown with enough force will break a glass window. In contrast, synchronicity has to do with *subjective* experience —if a person has a sudden premonition warning him or her to move away from a window and if seconds later a rock flies through it, the awareness of the premonition makes the broken window a synchronistic event. The timing is significant to the person, for whom the inner psychological premonitory feeling was in some unknown way linked to an outer event, which then followed.

To appreciate cause and effect, one needs the ability to observe outer events and to think logically. To appreciate a synchronistic event, one needs the ability to note an inner subjective state, a thought, feeling, vision, dream, or premonition and to intuitively link it with a related outer event. Synchronicity is a *co*-incidence of events that is meaningful to the participant; thus each synchronistic experience is unique. Causality is a sequence of events that can be logically explained and is generally repeatable.

Jung maintained that the collective unconscious or the archetypal layer of the unconscious (two terms for the same phenomenon) was involved in synchronistic events. While he agreed with Freud that we each have a personal unconscious that owes its existence to personal experience and would contain whatever was forgotten or repressed, Jung also described a deeper layer of the unconscious, which he called the *collective unconscious* and which he considered universal and inborn.

What the collective unconscious is and what archetypes are took Jung hundreds of pages to elaborate. Two volumes of his collected works—Volume 9, Part 1: *The Archetypes and the Collective Unconscious,* and Volume 9, Part 2: *Aion* —provide the nucleus of Jung's theory. So it is presumptuous, but necessary, to explain archetypes in a few paragraphs here, in order to show the relationship between archetypes and synchronicity.

Jung describes archetypes as "patterns of instinctual behavior," saying that "There are as many archetypes as there are typical situations in life. Endless repetition has engraved these experiences into our psychic constitution." Examples of archetypal situations are those such as birth and death, marriage, mother and child bonds, or heroic struggles. Themes of relationship and conflict raised in Greek tragedies, myths, or modern plays often concern archetypal situations. It is because they touch a common chord in us all that they have universal appeal. The common chord is this archetypal layer.

Yet another definition of archetypes that Jung uses refers to "primordial images," or archetypal figures that become activated and then clothed with personally derived emotional coloration. This occurs when an emotional situation develops that corresponds to a particular archetype. For example, a person may go to hear a lecture from an elderly man, whose presence and words evoke an emotional response to the archetype of the Wise Old Man. Immediately, that man becomes "numinous" or awesome; he is experienced as being wise and powerful; every word uttered by him seems charged with significance. Accepted as the Wise Old Man, whatever he says is not examined critically. Considered as a source of wisdom, his every word, however mundane, seems a pearl of wisdom. The archetype has become personified—clothed as this particular man, who is given all the attributes of the archetype. Other examples of archetypal figures are the divine child, all-giving mother, patriarchal father, temptress, or trickster—all are symbolic, recurring figures in dreams, literature, and religions.

When the archetypal level of the collective unconscious is touched in a situation, there is emotional intensity as well as a tendency for symbolic expression. Then the usual everyday level of experience becomes altered; there is more "magic" in the air, one can become "inspired," or be "on a crusade." Colloquial expressions acknowledge this change in psychological level: "What the devil got into him anyway?" or "He got caught in the grip of an idea" or "She went out of her mind with fear or rage."

When this emotionally charged archetypal level is active, then dream images of great intensity and symbolic meaning may arise, and synchronistic events are more likely to occur. Both dreams and synchronistic events are expressed symbolically, which shows their common connection in the collective unconscious. However, this does not "explain" how or why synchronicity occurs—it merely notes that there is a connection between synchronicity and an active archetype in the collective unconscious.

Jung described the relationship between the collective unconscious and synchronistic events in a 1945 letter to Dr. J. B. Rhine, the noted extrasensory perception researcher. Jung said that the collective unconscious behaved *"as if it were one and not as if it were split into many individuals"* and as manifesting itself *"not only in human beings but also at the same time in animals and even in physical conditions."* Jung then gave an example to illustrate this:

> I walked with a woman patient in the wood. She tells me about the first dream in her life that had made an everlasting impression on her. She had seen a spectral fox coming downstairs in her parental home. At this moment, a real fox comes out of the trees not forty yards away and walks quietly on the path ahead of us for several minutes. The animal behaves as if it were a partner in the situation.

This is one of those eerie synchronicities that seem to be saying that what is being discussed in that moment is highly emotionally charged and important. What the fox represented must have been a central issue in her family situation.

In his autobiography, *Memories, Dreams and Reflections*, Jung described the synchronistic event that had the greatest personal significance for him. It had occurred at the end of a lengthy and lonely period that followed his break with Freud. He had differed with Freud on a major premise, saying that incest was a symbolic rather than a literal problem, as Freud held. This "excommunicated" Jung from the psychoanalytic movement, leaving him without colleagues. Jung saw his patients, and continued to work on understanding the psyche in isolation. His theoretical differences brought his very significant friendship with Freud to an end and resulted in his expulsion from the professional community around Freud. He described this as *"a period of inner uncertainty, a state of disorientation."* It was a time when he had not yet found his own footing. Instead of listening to patients with a theory in mind, he resolved to listen to their dreams and fantasies with a completely open mind, merely asking them, "What occurs to you in connection with that?" or "How do you mean that, where does it come from, and what do you think about it?" He did the same with his own dreams, delved into his own childhood memories, and followed an impulse to build a miniature town at the edge of a lake while his thinking clarified. In exploring the contents from his un-conscious—his dreams, visions, and fantasies—he drew pic-tures and came across psychic material that was the same as found in children, mental patients, and mythic imagination. This repetition of motifs and images in individuals and in the world's literature pointed toward the concept of collectively held archetypes.

He then became engrossed with mandalas, which figure prominently in Eastern mystical religions and in the spon-taneous drawings of people in turmoil, and tried to under-stand what they symbolized. (Mandalas are drawings that have a center point, often a circle within a square.) The idea gradually emerged that the mandala represented a meaning-giving center of the personality—which Jung called the Self and which was for him, the goal of psychic development.

He conceptualized the Self as a midpoint related to both ego and unconscious, yet equivalent to neither; a source of energy that urges the person to "become what one is"; an archetype that provides a sense of order and meaning in the personality. In *Memories, Dreams, and Reflections,* he said that if the goal of psychological development is the Self then *"there is no linear evolution (except at the beginning of life); there is only the circumambulation of the self."*

While working on this concept, Jung had a dream about a well-fortified golden castle. He was painting this image in the center of a mandala, which was Chinese in feeling, when he received *The Secret of the Golden Flower* from Richard Wil-helm with a request that he write a commentary on it. Jung was moved by the event, which was a tremendously mean-ingful coincidence and writes,

I devoured the manuscript at once, for the text gave me undreamed-of confirmation of my ideas about the mandala and the circumambulation of the center. That was the first event which broke through my isolation. I became aware of an affinity, I could establish ties with something and someone. In remembrance of this coincidence, this synchronicity, I wrote underneath the picture which had made so Chinese an impression upon me: "In 1928, when I was painting this picture, showing the golden, well-fortified castle, Richard Wilhelm in Frankfurt sent me the thousand-year-old text on the yellow castle, the germ of the immortal body."

The break with Freud had occurred some sixteen years previously. Jung had during these years had no support for his ideas. To find in an ancient Chinese text a view that paralleled his own conceptions was confirmation of the value of his solitary studies into the nature of the psyche. This synchronistic event must have brought with it a sense that what he had been working on these many years, had meaning after all, dispelling doubts about the choices he had made. His theoretical differences had isolated him, and the decision to delve into the psyche had so preoccupied him that he had withdrawn from the university where he had lectured for eight years and had the expectation of a smooth academic career. This sense of isolation that had resulted from these choices was changed by the synchronistic event. Now he felt an affinity to others.

I think of Jung's circumambulation of the Self as paralleling the Eastern mind's effort to be in relationship to the Tao. Think of consciousness circling around a center, never being the same as the center, but being touched by the energy or divinity of it, as a planet circles the sun, warmed and illuminated by it—and the image, once more, is of the dance around the still point. *"At the still point of the turning world"*—where our consciousness or the worldliness of the ego, circles, turns, circumambulates—or dances around the eternal, infinite, inexpressible, indescribable, centering, meaning-giving principle. This still point in the center of the dance, is the *Tao* of the East and is the *Self* of Jung's psychology. The Self is usually felt as an inner perception of a numinous center, while the Tao—by giving us an awareness of an underlying oneness through which we are connected to everything in the universe—often seems to be outside of us. Both are versions of the same vision of reality and are interchangeable, recalling Frederick Franck's intuition *"that what is outside happens in me, that outside and inside are unseparated."* Tao and Self can be considered one and the same, both giving meaning and both beyond definition.

When considering the relationship between ego and Self, I suggest suspending a need to define where the Self exists in space. We Westerners are attached to the idea that everything "psychological" must be located in the space between our ears: Not making location an issue helps us understand the Self better. Sensing the existence of a divine energy *is* the experience. *Where* it exists is immaterial. Should we quibble about whether "God" is "out there," as in Browning's couplet *"God's in his heaven, / all's right with the world,"* or inside of us, as when we call it the Holy Spirit? What does it matter if we think of the Tao or of the Self— when the crucial similarity is the experience of grace in the moment, the source being beyond our comprehension and ineffable.

If synchronicity is indeed the Tao of psychology, how is it I am now interchanging the Self with the Tao? Metaphorically, I see the interchange as similar to the discovery in quantum physics that at the atomic level matter has a dual aspect—it appears as particles and as waves, depending on the situation—or similar to what Christians experience in the mystery of the Trinity, where God is one and yet is Father, Son, and Holy Spirit. Each are aspects of the same reality, viewed from a different perspective. Since our brains—our dominant left cerebral hemispheres specifically—have difficulty grasping totality, we experience parts of the whole picture and give each aspect a different name. The Self is what we experience inwardly when we feel a relationship to oneness, to the eternal Tao that connects everything outside of us to us. Synchronicity is felt through a specific coincidental event that is meaningful to us, through which the underlying Tao is revealed.

Synchronicity is the connecting principle (when cause and effect are eliminated by the impossibility of any rational explanation) between our psyches and an external event, in which we feel an uncanny sense of inner and outer being linked. In the experience of a synchronistic event, instead of feeling ourselves to be separated and isolated entities in a vast world we feel the connection to others and the universe at a deep and meaningful level. That underlying connection is the eternal Tao, and a synchronistic event is a specific manifestation of it.

CHAPTER 3

THE AGATHA CHRISTIE APPROACH TO SYNCHRONICITY

Detecting the significance of a synchronistic event · The inquiring attitude · Uncovering methods and seeking specific meaning · Synchronistic events as clues that we are invisibly connected to others and to the universe

To know that there will be no new Agatha Christie mysteries is sad. It's a bit like being a kid and having "Let's Pretend" go off the air, or watching the very last episode of "Star Trek" or "Upstairs, Downstairs." Until she died (and two more mysteries were even published posthumuously), Agatha Christie seemed to be an indefatigable English institution. Because she wrote her many mysteries year in and year out, I could enjoy reading her latest and anticipate that there would soon be another. It is something of a busman's holiday for a psychiatrist to read such mysteries, because her detectives, Hercule Poirot and Jane Marple, approach human situations in much the same fashion as does a psychiatrist. And in each book were events or objects about which Agatha Christie would ask, "What does this mean?" Or she would describe the character of a person and, since "Character is fate," the clue would be found in the personality pattern of victim or suspect.

To me, the Agatha Christie approach is intuitive; it asks "What is the meaning of this event?" "What are the circumstances in which it arose?" "What are the possibilities inherent in it?" In contrast, a more literal, concrete mind concerns itself mainly with the event or the thing itself—what it is now and what the five senses can take in of it. In order to see the total picture, both approaches are needed.

Taking an Agatha Christie approach to synchronistic events, one proceeds with an assumption that such events have meaning that can be "detected." For example, one of my patients, who knew I had an interest in psychic phenomena, began his session one day with what he considered an aside: an anecdote about a curious ESP event. Now, ESP always carries a "Gee whiz!" quality—it's like unexpectedly stumbling across something marvelous and fanciful. But to go beyond "Isn't it amazing?" to "What could it mean?" is the mystery to unravel in order to find personal relevance in the event.

He had been on a cruise ship in the Pacific when he had an apparently insignificant dream. In the dream, he was in Holland with a group of young men. They had gotten off a cruise ship, had taken a touring car out into the countryside, and now were piling back into the car to return to the ship. He was the last one still outside, when he saw a giant man wearing a Dutch boy's cap, striding toward him. His attention was riveted on the figure, which approached and walked on by. While my patient followed him with his eyes, the big man turned his head, and looked directly at my patient over his shoulder, with a strong inquiring gaze, as if to say "Will you follow me?" Meanwhile his dream friends were urging him to hurry up and get in the car. The dream ended there and he didn't consider it very significant.

The next day, in real life, the ship docked in Honolulu, where he was met by a friend. The friend suggested that they drop by the house of some friends of his, people my patient had neither met nor heard of before. As he walked into this house, he was struck by the strong Dutch influence in the decor. Then he looked over at the fireplace and saw a large painting of a Dutch man wearing the exact costume of the man in the dream, wearing the same cap, walking down a road, and peering back over his shoulder with the same look, having the same stance as in the dream. The only difference was that there was a woman at his side in the painting.

My patient was a bit jolted by the coincidence, feeling the spookiness of it all. But he didn't think to analyze its meaning. Like many ESP events, this precognitive dream elicited a sense of wonder and amazement.

Having an Agatha Christie attitude toward synchronicity, I proceeded on the assumption that the dream was especially important *because* it got underlined by the ESP event. That the symbolic Dutch man turned up twice warranted paying attention. Focusing on the dream with the assumption that it was an important "clue," we used amplification and active imagination to further understand it. "Amplification" is like asking the patient to look through a magnifying glass—to go into the details of the dream and to ask for associations to its elements, while the analyst may suggest other possible symbolic connections or potential meanings. In this simple and sketchy dream, the Dutch man was estimated to be about eight feet tall in relation to my six-foot tall patient—like a grown man would look to a boy. His companions in the car were stereotypes of affluent young men interested in adventures and good times.

In an active imagination, the person starts with an image of a person or place, animal, object, or symbol, often from a dream, and in a relaxed mental state "sees" or imagines what happens next. The image elaborates itself as a person observes. It can be like a waking dream. In this case, my patient found that the Dutch man was a patriarchal figure, in a large extended family or clan. He was a working man, as solid as a rock, reliable, dependable, and respected for his common-sense advice.

This giant man was presenting him a question crucial to his growth: "Will you follow me? Or will you stay with your companions?" Will you follow the patriarchal principle—will you grow up and be a man that others can look to for strength and dependability, or will you stay with your youthful companions in the cruise ship, seeking good times and more adventures? The choice was crucial and aptly presented: patriarchal principle or eternal youth—with which would he identify, which would he follow?

Following the assumption that the dream was especially important because of the ESP event, we uncovered its significance. The symbolic Dutch man was the major new archetype or symbol in his psyche. In the months that followed the dream, the dreamer acted decisively from strength. He felt an identification with his own father for the first time, even noticing and being pleased that his hands seemed to resemble those of his father.

Apparently trivial events can be synchronistic and taken further, when the significance is appreciated. For example, the morning I was to see a particular young woman I looked through my mail to find her check returned for insufficient funds. When she came in, aware that the check to me had been returned, she said, "I didn't want to talk about money, but I guess I'm going to have to." Money had been a very important but unspoken issue and one she had been reluctant to bring up. Now synchronicity seemed to require it and gave her the message that she couldn't avoid the subject. She had not had a check bounce in over three years. She had written some fifteen or twenty checks before and after the one for me, all of which had cleared the bank. *Only* her check to me had been returned for lack of funds. For her, this was a meaningful coincidence in which the outer event was connected to a highly emotional inner issue.

For most people, having checks returned is a predictable consequence of not putting enough money in the bank. The message is not mysterious, but is only a matter of shaping up in either the accounting or spending department. But when it is a "fluke event," then the Agatha Christie approach is to consider whether it is synchronistic and, if it is, what the significance might be. When her check bounced, the meaning to my patient was that she could not continue to duck the money issue. The cost of psychotherapy had galled her because she had trouble spending money on herself and because of the difficulty placing this much worth on her therapy with me. The synchronistic bounced check confronted her with the message that she couldn't run away from these important emotional issues.

Frederic Spiegelberg, the eminent scholar of comparative religion at Stanford and president of the Institute of Asian Studies in San Francisco, compares and contrasts an Easterner's attitude toward unexpected unfortunate events with a Westerner's reaction. In his classes at Stanford, Spiegelberg describes the difference between the Professor and the Pundit on being hit by a falling brick while crossing the campus. The Professor, on being struck by the brick, which breaks his arm, calls out in pain and surprise, attracting students who gather around. Prompt medical help is sought. Then the area is cordoned off while maintenance is called. The university is held responsible, and its insurance company will pay for the accident. The Professor meanwhile feels it was an unlucky event and is angry or sorry for himself, feeling magnaminous if he doesn't sue. Other people commiserate as they sign his cast, considering it either the school's fault or something no one could have foreseen.

The Pundit, on crossing the campus and being struck by the falling brick, does not call out and attract attention to his broken arm, as he considers the event a reflection on himself, an effect of some of his deserved karma. Instead, he immediately starts examining himself to see what he has done to cause such a thing. The idea of protecting others from further falling bricks or of expecting insurance coverage does not enter his mind. He assumes himself to be at fault and also takes no responsibility for anyone else.

For the Professor, such an untoward event comes out of the blue. He was an innocent passer-by and has played no part in its occurrence. For the Pundit, everything that happens to him is considered totally deserved, and therefore he feels wholly responsible for the broken arm.

A person who understands that synchronicity does occur but who also believes that it is *not* the only operating principle would probably first react like the Professor and then reflect on the event like the Pundit. He or she would not assume fault for the event, while considering the possibility of synchronicity. Applying an Agatha Christie approach, the person would look at the event as a potential meaningful coincidence, asking "Is it 'commenting' on an inner situation? Is it a metaphor for something going on in my life?" When we accept the idea of synchronicity, every unusual event invites us to to pause and reflect on it.

This attitude of seeking the possible meaning or potential significance can be applied both in ordinary life and in psychotherapy, to dreams and to synchronistic events. Both are events in which the collective unconscious is manifested in symbolic language. People often overlook or forget them and first need to notice and remember such events and dreams. Then they can consider the potential meanings by thinking about the symbolic elements and by wondering whether these elements seem analogous to anything currently important or troublesome.

Often the meaning is not altogether clear; however, the process itself is valuable even when a fitting interpretation does not result. The value lies in feeling connected to the collective, symbolic unconscious, which is subjectively nourishing. When a person who has been remembering dreams "loses them" and goes through a period of dream impoverishment, the experience is that of being out of touch with something important, of being disconnected from a meaning-giving source.

Given our limited consciousness, which can only "see" a portion of the collective unconscious at a time, symbols or impressions from dreams or synchronistic events are very often only partially understood, through hints followed by guesses. Sometimes, when a series of unusual events happens one may get a feeling, which grows with each new addition, that "Something is trying to tell me something." Maybe the indicator is hair standing up on the back of the neck, or a "pricking of the thumbs"—whatever the signal, one feels that a message needs to be deciphered. The Agatha Christie approach is then a very natural one.

My painter friend, Ann Hogle, was struck by just such a

series of events. Her son had thought of a practical joke he wanted to play in Latin class the next day and persuaded her to go with him to sign for some "blanks" at the gun shop. He and a friend wanted to fire a gun at a crucial point in the class. On the way back home, at the foot of the hill, they came across the results of a very recent accident in which a car had been completely gutted by fire. The scene was terrible. At home that afternoon, a fire burst out on top of the stove, the coffee grounds caught fire, were put out, and then were vacuumed up. Then the vacuum cleaner caught fire (apparently some coffee grounds had been smoldering inside). These were the only two fires ever to happen in her house. That evening, my friend watched TV only briefly and found she was watching a film of a fire. Troubled, feeling a repetition of fire was significant, she looked up "fire" in a dictionary of symbols. But still she achieved no understanding of the possible meaning of these events. She then went to sleep, troubled and puzzled, and awoke at 4:00 AM, convinced that the fires must have something to do with firing the blanks.

In the morning, she talked to her son, saying that she would rather he didn't fire the gun. Although she had no logical reason to connect the series of fires to this event, it intuitively seemed to be connected. Her son readily agreed, having sensed the weirdness of the events. Later, during the Latin class in which he had intended to fire the blanks, ear-splitting explosions were heard in the hall right outside the classroom. Two boys had been fooling around with firecrackers, which had exploded; the hands of one boy had been injured.

What to make of an event like this? What would have happened if she hadn't felt warned? Did this firecracker explosion take the place of something that would otherwise have happened? And if so, why? Being used to neatly packaged solutions to Agatha Christie mysteries, this one leaves me unsatisfied and unsettled. My friend, however, derives a sense of meaning in it, feeling that the firecracker episode was the important touch through which she felt the impact of the sequence of events.

This series of synchronistic events leaves the logical mind

unsatisfied, but her intuitive mind, which participated in it, had a deep-seated conviction (which words do not convey adequately) of having experienced that underlying cosmic reality—that Tao. My friend did not need thought or theory to "rationalize" the experience—the synchronistic series of events itself was clearly significant enough.

Telepathic communication provides another example in which the feelings evoked by the synchronistic experience seem more important than any specific message conveyed by the event. Recently, two women told me about receiving such messages—in their cases, literally "gut-level communication."

One was Judy Vibberts, who had been having an uneventful, pleasantly relaxed afternoon in Golden Gate Park, when precisely at 4:30 (she unaccountably noted the time) sudden excruciating, doubling-up abdominal pain struck out of the blue, accompanied by a splitting headache. That evening, she found out that a good friend had been in a terrible accident. Her side of the car had been smashed in, and she had severe abdominal and head injuries. She had been taken immediately to a hospital, needed emergency surgery to remove her ruptured spleen, and was on the critical list in the intensive care unit. The accident had occurred at exactly 4:30 PM, and the "message" was sent instantaneously to Judy, who picked up the information viscerally in this telepathic manner.

Nancy Haugen was similary "struck" by a painful message. This time it was a mother-to-daughter communication transmitted across an entire continent. Her mother in Philadelphia developed an "acute abdomen," cause initially not certain, with vomiting and retching as the most predominant symptoms, along with cramping pain. The picture eventually pointed to an obstruction requiring surgery. Meanwhile, Nancy, in northern California, seemed to have had "sympathic vibrations," in her gastrointestinal system. Before her father telephoned to tell her what was happening, Nancy spent several uncomfortable hours with a sensation in her body of having "the heaves," but without throwing up.

Telepathic events usually occur between two people who

have a deeply felt bond—between parent and child, spouses, lovers, good friends, and especially between twins. They seem intuitively tuned in to each other through an emotional connection in which love is the most common bond. Perhaps, when we love, something is imprinted in the psyche, so that we are open to send and receive on a particular channel keyed to that relationship. The "medium" through which these messages are sent and received I think of as the collective unconscious, which connects us all. (Some mediumistic individuals seem to be able to tune in to this level and to scan it for information without requiring a particularly important emotional bond, but almost all other spontaneously arising telepathic events occur between two individuals with a deep emotional connection).

Now, a deep connection must also occur for the analytic process to be effective: The relationship touches elements in the personal and collective unconscious of both analyst and patient. Because synchronicity involves the collective unconscious and because telepathic communication can occur between two people who share an emotional bond, it would seem to follow that the therapeutic relationship is one in which ESP or synchronistic events between analyst and patient might occur. And in fact that is the case. Jung observed that *"The relationship between doctor and patient, especially when a transference on the part of the patient occurs, or in more or less unconscious identification of doctor and patient, can lead to parapsychological phenomena."* In one instance, he described a viscerally received telepathic connection between himself and his patient. Jung had traveled to deliver a lecture and returned to his hotel about midnight. He had gone to bed and had lain awake for a long time, and then: *"At about two o'clock—I must have just fallen asleep—I awoke with a start, and had the feeling that someone had come into the room; I even had the impression that the door had been hastily opened. I instantly turned on the light, but there was nothing. Someone might have mistaken the door, I thought, and I looked into the corridor. But it was still as death. 'Odd,' I thought, 'Someone did come into the room!' Then I tried to recall exactly what had happened, and it occurred to me that I had been awakened by a feeling of dull pain, as though something had struck my forehead and then the back of my skull. The following day I received a telegram saying that my patient had committed suicide. He had shot himself. Later I learned that the bullet had come to rest in the back wall of his skull."*

The patient rather than the doctor may be the receiver in a telepathic exchange. A colleague of mine described such a situation. She had left her practice in San Francisco to go on a month-long trip to the Mid-East and Europe—a vacation that was brought to an abrupt end by a tragedy: the double suicide of her parents. Because they had lived on the East Coast, and the event had taken place in Israel, no word of it had been reported in San Francisco. My colleague returned as previously scheduled to resume her work with patients. She thought that telling them the details of what had happened would unnecessarily burden them, while behaving as if she were merely returning from her long vacation would be a detrimental pretense. So she decided to tell them only that her planned vacation had been cut short by a tragedy in her family. A patient then reported a dream in which she was traveling in a bus with her therapist (her therapist was with relatives) when the bus began to fill with poison gas. Since the double death of her parents was through carbon monoxide, it seemed to my colleague that her patient had picked up on details of her emotional situation and incorporated them into a dream.

It is difficult to ascertain where intuition ends and telepathy begins when two people are in conversational rapport. In the analytic process, it often seems as if doctor and patient are in a mild, shared, light trance state. Face to face in separate chairs, they unconsciously mirror each other's body position and gestures, while at the same time deeply sharing material and feelings. In such situations, I often think of something, and my patient's next words are about it. Or a dream may be described, and it seems as if my mental image and the dream image must be similar because the dream situation is so readily understood. (Once Harry Wilmer, then a Professor of Psychiatry at Langley Porter Institute, proposed getting an artist to reproduce what the patient saw and what the therapist saw, to check out whether this subjective feeling of "seeing" the same dream image were true and then to see what the feeling might mean. But as far as I know that has not been done.) A research group of four Jungian analysts in Berlin has been noting the occurrence of synchronistic events in the analytic process; in *Success and Failure in Analysis,* Hans Dieckmann reports on their findings. Their examples focus on extrasensory perceptions that arise during analytic sessions when archetypal material is present. The therapist may have what he or she feels to be an "extraneous" mental image, only to find it is very significant to the patient. Or a patient's dream may trigger highly personal memories and thoughts in the therapist, which lead him or her, surprisingly, to understanding the images in the patient's dream. At times therapist and patient seem connected by a telepathic bond or seem to have an interwoven shared psyche. This depth of connection has also been felt by most people outside of a psychiatrist's office, when one person is speaking about a deeply moving, important, and private experience to another who understands by making feeling connections to his or her own similar experiences, when each is sharing events that can be visually imagined and emotionally felt by the other.

All these examples of synchronicity are "clues" or singular events, interesting in and of themselves. By taking an Agatha Christie approach to them, we can see what the pattern of these clues points to or suggests about the underlying meaning of these events.

A synchronistic event may become symbolically meaningful when our understanding of the symbol present in the event gives us insight into our personal psychological situations. Working with synchronistic events as if they were dreams and unraveling their symbolic meanings can be as valuable as working with dreams. To me, telepathy between two people is evidence of their connection at the deeper level of the collective unconscious, through bonding that may be either biological or psychological. When it occurs in therapy, it is a measure of the existence of transference and countertransference, or of a loving connection, or both. The event indicates how deeply the work is reaching.

Each of these events are clues intimating the possibility that we and everything in the universe might be invisibly linked, rather than unrelated and separate, providing supporting evidence for the existence of an underlying matrix or Tao. For synchronicity to happen, the space between individuals and things, rather than being empty, must somehow "contain" a connecting link or be a transmission medium. Jung calls this the *collective unconscious.*

Synchronistic events are the *clues* that point to the existence of an underlying connecting principle. Whenever synchronicity occurs, the visible and tangible "ten thousand things" are experienced as being aspects of the one, while the invisible matrix, that inexpressible, ineffable, unseen connection; the Tao, is the the great mystery.

CHAPTER 4

LIKE A WAKING DREAM

Synchronistic events are like dreams · Central casting works well · Symbolic interpretation as a means of understanding the synchronistic incident

As an "oldie but goodie" song begins, "Have you ever seen a dream walking? Well, I have." Whether dreamboat or nightmare, a synchronistic event can be like a dream that happens to you when you are awake. Like dreams, such events are related to the concerns of the psyche, are usually metaphorical comments about something psychologically important, and can provide insight into the situation when they are understood. A synchronistic event may be instantaneously charged with significance or may require a pause to reflect on its possible significance. Similarly, some dreams seem immediately important and clear in their meaning, but most need to be analyzed for the message. Furthermore, the tools through which the meaning of the synchronicity can be understood are the same ones that work in dream interpretation.

As with the experience of dreaming, synchronicity shows tremendous variation from person to person. Some people remember dreaming every night; others claim they never dream. Some remember only having a few important dreams in their whole lives, and the few they remember they may have dreamed in childhood. Some people have dreams full of symbols and color; others report having dreams in shades of grays or filled with everyday trivia. So also with synchronicity: Some people notice synchronicity occurring around them almost every day, while others cannot ever remember having such a meaningful coincidence. Still others have had one or two really significant synchronistic events in their lives, which made a lasting impression. Recall, frequency, intensity, dramatic quality of synchronistic events vary as much as with dreams, and the repetitive themes that recur in synchronistic events can be like repetitive dreams. While central casting can be as imaginative and as precise in synchronistic events as in dreams.

Since the variation is so very great when people are asked either about their dreams or the occurrence of synchronicity, it is interesting to speculate about the discrepancy between recall and actuality. When William Dement (the noted researcher of the stages of sleep) and his associates at Stanford University studied dreaming, they found that, regardless of what we remember, all of us dream between six to eight times every night. I venture the intuitive opinion that this is true of synchronicity as well—that, whether we notice it or not, synchronistic events are occurring around us every day.

The individual variations may have to do with personality characteristics. It seems to me that people who have the most difficulty recalling dreams—or relating to them when they can remember them—tend to be logical, overly rational, work-focused people; more often men than women; people who have been called "heart-attack prone personalities," with uptight, unplayful minds. For this kind of person, the concept of synchronicity is highly suspect, to be discounted along with ESP or mystical religious experience. Lacking an intuitive way of knowing, they rarely experience the awareness that something can have spiritual meaning or psychological significance. Dreams and synchronistic events thus are less likely to have an impact on them and be remembered, and, when remembered, are felt to have no significance.

Like dreams, synchronicity depends on the activity of the psyche. A person in great inner turmoil quite often recalls dreams of great intensity, unusually vivid and emotionally charged, and dream recall also rises. Synchronicity also seems to increase in some dimension when there is intensity of feeling, whether that feeling be due to falling in love, or being in a period of creative struggle, or meeting a heightened state of emotional conflict. With increased emotional tension, synchronistic events seem to be more frequent, ESP incidents increase, and using the *I Ching,* which relies on synchronicity, often produces uncannily precise readings. Possibly the increase in psychological intensity produces more effects, or perhaps the emotional turmoil is disorienting, so that the individual pays greater attention to dreams and synchronicity.

Like dreams, which seem to have been put together with the expert help of some sort of central casting, in choosing a particular person or symbol to represent something, so may the synchronistic event have an equally imaginative or even humorously precise choice of elements. For the following example of the high quality of "central casting" and to show how a synchronistic event can be interpreted and worked with like a dream, I go back to a dinner party conversation.

Dinner was over and we had regrouped in a room with a large sliding glass door that looked out over a green lawn, past bushes and a fence to the rolling, brown, grass-covered hills of Tiburon. Three couples drinking coffee and brandy, talking. Ann, an artist, raised a personally perplexing question that engaged us all. She described the occasional experience of closing her eyes and then seeing images of demoniac, evil faces. She would instinctively recoil and by opening her eyes, break contact with whatever they were or whatever they represented. Then she would wonder if instead she should have confronted them in some way. Was this shutting them off cowardly? Was it psychologically wrong to avoid this?

As three of us were psychiatrists, another also an artist, and Jim, my husband, then editor and publisher of *Psychic* Magazine (now called *New Realities*), her question interested us from many angles, and we raised intellectual premises for either having more contact (through active imagination or dialogue) or avoiding them as she was doing. In the middle of this discussion, a sound intruded, that of an animal scratching at the sliding glass door.

The noise distracted us. We turned to see a skunk trying to get in. The focus of our conversation naturally turned to this unusual situation. This was the first skunk that our hosts had ever seen in their vicinity. Skunks usually avoid people —why was this one trying to get in? Much laughter at the thought that anyone of us would get up to let it in. The evening ended shortly thereafter, as it was getting late.

When we were driving home, Jim raised the possibility that the skunk at the door was a synchronistic answer to Ann's question. Until that point, the event was just an unusual happening, of interest in itself and without meaning. (This was also how I used to feel, before my analysis, about my own dreams, which were in technicolor and had a semblance of a plot. For me, they were of passing interest, like going to the "flicks" or movies each night, notable only if something unusual had turned up.) By considering synchronicity, the event of the skunk at the door took on significance. Amazingly, an analogy to Ann's situation and the answer were both present in the event.

In wanting to get in, the skunk was like the demoniac faces. It would have been foolish to open the door—wisdom and common sense, not cowardice, would govern the decision. Letting the skunk in would contaminate and stink up the living space, metaphorically suggesting that letting in the demoniac images with a negative energy would do the same to one's inner space. Central casting for this synchronistic event provided a vivid symbol. Thinking about the context and attributes of the symbol, suggested insight into Ann's situation and a subsequent choice of action, namely continued avoidance.

To understand a synchronistic event, or a dream, one can

first ask about the emotional context in which it occurred. What was troublesome? What was the problem in need of solution? What was the state of affairs, or inner mood and outer circumstance? Synchronistic events seem to occur within an emotional context, commenting on and paralleling the real-life situation. In the example of the skunk, the event was an immediate, simultaneous commentary by analogy.

Next it is helpful to wonder what the people, animals, or things involved in the event might symbolize (a skunk is pretty obvious) and what analogous meaning the event might have.

Sometimes a synchronistic event is disturbingly obvious to the person involved. Having her dog hit by a car had immediate, eerie meaning to one woman, as it happened just after she had separated from the man she had been living with. Only once previously had she ever owned a dog, and it had been stolen from her car immediately following her decision not to marry the man she had then lived with. The first time, she had clearly ended the relationship, and that dog was never found. This time, separation had occurred over differences in values and lifestyles, and, although the survival of the relationship was in doubt, it was not yet dead. The dog, too, was still alive. She had a back injury and was dragging her hind legs and tail. If she didn't improve, she would have to be put to sleep. If the spinal cord had been severed (thus permanently separated) the dog could not recover, but if the paralysis were only temporary, and due to pressure, recovery was possible. As it turned out, both the dog and the relationship survived. The dog's spinal cord had not been severed, and this particular separation was only temporary.

A synchronistic meeting between people often can be viewed as similar to a waking dream in which a person encounters a symbol who gives direction or resolves a conflict. Sometimes a person has a dream in which a situation is "symbolically solved," and he or she may awaken with a new attitude that resolves the tension. Similarly a person may encounter another person in a synchronistic meeting who is like a living symbol: the effect of such a meeting seems to reach into the deeper levels of the psyche, to bring up new energy, which then becomes a decisive force in life.

An example of such an emotionally decisive synchronistic meeting occurred in the life of a woman professional, who had been mired for several months in indecision. She wanted to quit her work as a psychotherapist in order to have a child and work as an artist once again. Yet at every thought of doing this her anxiety would mount. First one side and then the other would dominate her thinking, with no resolution. Much as she wanted to be a mother, she did not want to be financially dependent on anyone, even her husband. This feeling was rooted to the economic difficulties her mother and she had been thrown into on her father's untimely death. At that time she had turned away from a very promising beginning in art to choose a professional career that offered more financial certainty.

Now the circumstances were quite different. She had returned to painting a little, enough to rekindle her old love for it, and she felt ready to have a baby. She saw this was clearly what she wanted to do, but she balked at bringing it about. She would have to phase out her private practice as a therapist in order to be mother and artist, and some part of her was afraid that this would mean giving up her professional life and her independence forever. She was in an intense quandary, caught between what she wanted to do now and her fear that she would be sorry later.

Sometimes in such circumstances a "big" dream comes along that helps resolve the situation, but in her case what happened was a synchronistic meeting. She had gone to an all-day symposium and had happened to sit next to a former colleague she had not seen for seven or eight years. They had both worked in the same agency, but had gone in different directions. At lunch, they began catching up with each other and filling in the blank of intervening time. As she listened to the other woman, she found herself responding deeply with a rush of joy and a sudden feeling of liberation from her tension, as she felt herself released from the immobilizing conflict she had been in.

She found that her colleague had dropped out professionally for six years to have a baby and be a nonworking, at-home mother. She had grown a large garden, baked bread, and fully lived an unhurried domestic life in a semirural setting. During this time, she had also become a potter. Now she was back in her professional life and was working and doing some teaching at the medical center.

Meeting this woman was like meeting a symbol that imbued her strong maternal urge with an element of faith. She felt the synchronicity of it intuitively; she knew that the meeting was uncannily significant. Synchronistic events impart a sense of being part of a greater whole; in meetings such as this, they can even convey the feeling that one is saying yes to destiny by heeding the message in the event. The impact of this meeting was so immediate that she left the symposium half way through, went home, threw her contraceptives out, and spent the afternoon making love with her husband.

While synchronistic meetings can have this kind of impact, when the symbolic level of the encounter is immediately felt, sometimes awareness of the synchronicity of an encounter is gradual, and the insight into its meaning also comes slowly. I have in mind the experience of a lawyer who was having career difficulties. Here the synchronistic meeting occurred over many months and took the form of an unappreciated, drawn-out struggle with another attorney—who personified his "shadow" or the inner, negative, self-defeating aspect or dark side of himself.

He described to me feelings of languishing in a job as a corporate lawyer, doing very routine and unchallenging work, with no future promise except more of the same. He had been considered outstanding at one of the highest ranked law schools in the country and had been offered and taken a position in a major law firm on graduation. He proceeded to show brilliance at litigation, winning cases against experienced men of noted reputation. Subsequently he left that firm and tried a few other possibilities before ending up where he was now. He felt defeated and stuck, and considered his job and work mediocre. He was also depressed and easily irritated; he felt that he took out his frustrations on his family, coming home to them crabby and resentful, no fun to be around.

When he was at work, he put up a façade—looking busy when he was just passing the time. Like Walter Mitty, he fantasized being somewhere else doing more interesting, heroic, and appreciated work, while the routine galled him and his self-contempt grew.

In time, he began to see that he had a personal priority he was ignoring: He had a need for excellence. Even given this need and his considerable abilities, achievement had eluded him. The search for an explanation turned up a strong self-defeating inner attitude, which depreciated and undermined his efforts. This was a shadowy presence in his psyche, an element with a cynical adolescent's attitude toward work and accomplishment, which sabotaged and thwarted any feelings of success.

After realizing what his personal priorities were, he acted decisively and rapidly. He resigned from his corporate position, and became an active partner in a small and struggling firm, where his abilities as a litigator could lead the firm to success. As he did this, he knew also that this decision could be undermined by his inner negativity. He knew he would fail if he didn't confront and overcome the tendency either to put down what he was doing when he got involved in work or to goof off, daydream, and make excuses.

Now feeling he was ready to confront his self-defeating tendencies, he unexpectedly and synchronistically had an encounter with a personification of all his negative traits. This man was an office associate, another attorney whom he met when he plunged into his new situation. On the surface, the other man seemed charming and intelligent, quite likable. Although he looked busy, he turned out to be unproductive, not even covering the overhead cost of having him there. He was depressed, putting off work and then making excuses. My patient found himself obsessively focusing on this man, overly disturbed, as he felt that the whole firm would be dragged down by him. Then he began to appreciate that he was obsessively focusing on this man as such an important make-or-break element because this man was a living, breathing, walking, talking symbol of his own inner negativity, which he confronted daily in his office. Perhaps this repeated synchronicity took the place of nightly dreams in which he might instead have struggled with a threatening dark man, who might have represented the struggle with this negative "shadow" element in himself.

His struggle to confront the outer man was the same as his inner struggle to master the sabotaging efforts of his shadow. Finally, he devised a way to get this man out of the office; by gradually giving him less and less work to do—a solution based on knowing what is negative within oneself and deciding to give it less and less energy until "it" goes. At the point the other man left, synchronistically, my patient had mastered his own negative adolescent attitude. He was now fully involved in his work, committed to building the firm, and was effectively working and carrying responsibility.

The difference between a synchronistic meeting that is immediately felt as significant, its meaning seen in an intuitive flash, and the more slowly evolving situation of this example, where both insight and resolution occur over a period of time, is very similar to what happens in doing dream interpretation in analysis. Since both dreams and synchronicity have a connection with the collective unconscious, it isn't surprising that working with dreams is very similar to working with synchronicity.

Sometimes a person has a highly emotional dream whose meaning is immediately evident and leads to a decisive act. More usually, though, a dreamer struggles repetitively with the same issues, gradually understanding what the dream events are about, gaining insight into the nature of the conflict before change comes about. Dream themes that are uncomfortable and repetitive usually continue until the inner psychological conflict or the conflicting external situation changes. Synchronistic events follow the same pattern.

For example, one woman had three auto accidents in a row —rather like having repetitive, bad, waking dreams. She had a blemish-free insurance record, yet found herself saying, "It's me again" to the claims adjustor. In each case, she was apparently blameless. The first time, she was in a center lane, stopped and waiting for a light to change, when she heard a squealing, skidding sound. The street was slick, wet with the first seasonal rain; another woman had braked too late and crashed into the rear of her car. In the second accident, she was driving in a middle lane, going with the flow of traffic, when a woman suddenly changed lanes and swerved into her, (either because she wasn't looking or because of a blind spot). In the third accident, just as in the first, she had stopped in a middle lane, waiting for a light to change, when the impact of another rear-end collision hurled her car into the intersection. This time, a young woman's brakes had failed, and she had rammed into the back of the car, rupturing the gas tank and creating a potentially explosive situation.

What should she make of this? No causal explanation would explain this sequence. Was it pure chance, bad luck, or synchronicity?

The first accident had seemed to be a metaphor for what was deeply troubling her: A woman co-worker had recently made an emotional impact, and the intense feelings had been jarring (a situation that might have been caused by not putting the brakes on feelings soon enough). The possibility of synchronicity in the second accident was also considered and ignored. The third accident was, however, absolutely convincing: On the same day as the last accident (in which she was hit by a woman whose brakes had failed), her co-worker's car brakes also failed. After that, it was clearly time to accept the accidents as synchronistic events that were commenting on the situation. The accidents were like a series of dreams in which the same theme repeated itself in different settings until the dreamer got the message, and acknowledged that the relationship was mutually damaging. It was time to stop trying to be friends.

The coincidental timing and symbolic quality of such events convince people of synchronicity. The coincidence is between a psychological situation and an outer accident, meeting, or event—in which the outer situation is a symbolic representation of the psychological struggle or conflict. It seems to me that synchronicity is frequent, but unless an individual has some insight into the psychological situation the symbolic coincidence is not appreciated. Like ignored dreams, they have no impact.

Sometimes a dream and an outer event reverberate together, creating the synchronicity. For example, a psychiatrist dreamed that he carefully pruned his Japanese maple tree. The dreamer, a multitalented man who was in analysis with me, saw this task as a metaphor for what he needed to do. He had been expending his energy in several directions, which took him away from his life work. The Japanese maple, a symbol of his inner, deeper self which he had come to know through me, needed to be pruned of these lesser offshoots so that the main trunk would grow strong. The next weekend, as he in actuality pruned and shaped this maple, aware of the symbolic meaning of the task—tingles went up his spine, as a feeling of numinosity filled him with a sense of awe, mystical awareness, and joy. This was a Tao experience through synchronicity, as sleeping dream and waking dream coincided in meaning.

Paying attention to synchronicity, like paying attention to dreams, adds an extra dimension that enriches our inner lives and adds another facet to our awareness. In order to understand ourselves and the situation around us, we are far better off if we can receive and process information from symbolic as well as from logical sources. Because thinking and five sense perceptions are processed in one cerebral hemisphere and because symbolic, intuitive functions seem to be located in the other, when we consider input from both logical and symbolic sources we can see the whole picture. Our perceptions about the nature of the situation and our decisions about the attitude or action to take then can be based on what we know or feel intuitively as well as on rational considerations.

Since synchronicity resembles dreams in so many ways, it is no surprise to find that the same warnings about the dangers of becoming all too engrossed or fascinated by dreams also apply to synchronicity. The potential one-sidedness of focusing solely on dreams or on synchronicity, involves an abdication of logical thinking and reality testing. When we get lost in this way, magical thinking dominates us and we look for omens and base our actions on them. Such one-sidedness also limits the range of information available to assess and process.

Similarly, relying only on linear thinking and perception through the five senses (sight, hearing, smell, touch, taste) is equally impoverishing. It can result in a personal experience that is devoid of emotional meaning and lacks imaginative or spiritual dimensions. We need an intuitive, feeling, emotional component to appreciate music, art, and symbolic experiences. Synchronicity, like dreams, invites us to participate in the symbolic level, where we sense there is underlying meaning, where we share a collective unconscious with humanity, where time and space become relative, and where, in the course of our everyday lives, we experience a nonordinary reality.

Synchronicity is like a waking dream in which we experience the point of intersection of the timeless with time, where the impossible union of spheres of existence is actual, and where what is inside of us and what is outside of us is unseparated. Like a dream, synchronicity reveals something we dimly grasp, glimpses of the underlying Tao.

CHAPTER 5

SIGNIFICANT MEETINGS AND THE SYNCHRONISTIC MATCHMAKER

*"Accidental" meetings that
lead to significant relationships · Synchronicity at work
as the matchmaker · Inner archetypes and outer people*

Synchronicity can pave the way for people coming together. By unraveling the circumstances through which two people meet to enter a *significant* relationship, the delicate unseen hand of fate, destiny, synchronicity, or underlying Tao—by whatever name the matchmaker is called—can be discerned. When an accidental meeting brought about by apparent chance corresponds to an inner psychological situation, then it is a meaningful coincidence—where synchronicity is evident. It has worked thus for me in both my personal and my professional lives.

Just before I met my husband, for example, I had been feeling that a phase of my life was over and that it was time to move on. I responded to this inner state by deciding to actually move. I arranged to leave San Francisco and move to New York city to complete my last year of psychiatric residency before going on to London for a postresidency year. Just before I made the move, a chance meeting changed the course of my life.

Thanksgiving was coming up, and I decided to go to Los Angeles for the holiday. One of my roommates, Elaine Fedors, had been planning a Thanksgiving party in our Sausalito apartment. This party had been inspired by Dick Rawson, a psychiatric resident who had wanted to introduce a friend of his to Elaine. Two days before Thanksgiving, I found out that I was expected to be at the San Francisco clinic the Friday afterward, making a long Los Angeles weekend impossible. I was "grounded" and would be in Sausalito for the party after all. As a consequence, I met James Bolen, whom I married six months later. Coincidentally, Jim had also planned to have Thanksgiving with relatives in the Los Angeles area, when he unexpectedly had to remain in San Francisco because of work. Consequently at a loss for Thanksgiving plans, Jim called Dick to see if the invitation extended and declined some weeks before was still open. It was, and that's how Jim came into my life.

Dick and Jim had been in the Air Force together as young enlisted men, some twelve years before. After all those years intervening, they had just crossed paths again. In the interim, Jim had gone from engineering into journalism and public relations, moving in the process from Iowa to Southern California before coming to the San Francisco Bay area; Dick had gone from Berkeley to medical school in Los Angeles and then to Philadelphia before returning to San Francisco.

For Jim and me to have met at all took a complex series of coincidences. Our inner readiness for such a meeting through which love would grow rapidly into marriage also had required a number of twists and turns and other relationships to reach this significant intersection. It changed the course of both our lives, and our paths merged from then on.

Whether this was synchronicity at work or just the way things worked out is impossible to say. Retrospectively, it seems to me that the timing was significant, that I'd outgrown a long phase I'd been in and had ended a lengthy conflicted relationship, and was now ready to meet "a grown-up man." An outer, synchronistically arranged event coincided with my inner change and paralleled a similarly timed situation within Jim as well.

When two people meet synchronistically, each person is "a significant other," and both are at a critical personal juncture and capable of being deeply affected, then dramatic changes can result. As Jung says, *"The meeting of two personalities is like the contact of two chemical substances: If there is any reaction, both are transformed."* In some instances, each personality at that exact moment in time may be unusually susceptible to the particular "chemical" action of the other.

Reflect on your own significant meetings—those that led to intense, important relationships, a new career, or intellectual, psychological, or spiritual growth. Think about the people you have met who in one way or another changed the direction of your life profoundly. Then remember the circumstances of the initial meeting with each person. Was the encounter timely from an inner psychological point of view? Would you have been unreceptive or unavailable a short time before? Was there a new openness or susceptibility that corresponded to this new person? Could synchronicity have been the matchmaker? Significant meetings have resulted when two cars accidentally collided, or as a result of becoming lost in a foreign city and bumping into another American, or of randomly being seated next to one another on a Boeing 747 jet—all obviously unintentional, unplanned meetings that revealed the fine hand of synchronicity. When inner timing and outer meeting show a precise fit, when a meeting seems uncannily tailored and impossible to have arranged deliberately, then synchronicity may be the matchmaker at work.

Many synchronistic meetings seem to take place in my professional life. They are perhaps more obvious because the way in which a person reaches me (or any therapist) can be traced by a zig-zag route that may have been filled with coincidences. Synchronicity may also play a part in creating an opening in my schedule at just the right time to allow me to see a particular person. A new patient can be stirred deeply by the feeling that an extraordinary set of synchronistic circumstances have brought about the meeting with me, by a sense of specialness or purposefulness in the encounter. When this feeling is added to the powerful expectations and need that surround the event of seeing a psychiatrist for the first time, all these elements contribute to an intense therapeutic situation in which images and feelings are readily touched.

One particularly uncanny match occurred when an Episcopalian priest came to see me. I was the psychiatrist of a friend in whom he had confided his despair and anxiety, and I was the only psychiatrist about whom he knew—on the surface, an ordinary enough referral. This man had considerable difficulty trusting women and had been reluctant to call me until the increasing desperation of his situation finally forced him to overcome his reservations. He found it hard to imagine seeing a woman psychiatrist. Knowing me only as Dr. Jean Bolen, and assuming that I would be a Caucasian from my name, he sat in the waiting room fearing this appointment was a terrible mistake. Then I came down the stairs, and he unexpectedly met a five-foot-tall Japanese-American woman, which altered the situation remarkably.

The only positive feminine image of women that he had—thanks to an idolized uncle's stories from being in the American army of occupation in Japan—was that of a Japanese woman. He otherwise thought of women as being artificial and manipulative, vaguely hostile, powerful individuals who waited for an opening to be critical. Foreign to his own experience, but symbolizing the idea that a woman might be unthreatening, caring, supportive, and helpful in the midst of this overwhelming negative impression of women, was the Japanese woman about whom his uncle had told him.

Of course, on meeting me he was greatly relieved at the unexpected turn of events that made me someone with whom he could work after all. His initial relief later gave way to wonder, as the synchronicity of it all became further evident. He needed to delve into both his spiritual vocation and his creative strivings to write, and of all available therapies the Jungian perspective (which he had not consciously sought) was the most helpful in these areas. It seemed to him that a female, Japanese, Jungian psychiatrist was precisely what he needed. If so, synchronicity had to have been finely tuned to have arranged our meeting, since I was the only Japanese woman Jungian analyst to be found anywhere.

Another initial meeting that had the flavor of synchronicity led to my analysis of an artist who would be particularly significant for me. She had been given my name a few months before and, not knowing anything about me, did not call for an appointment, but carried my name on a slip of paper around with her. Some time later her mother, in Southern California, asked her to be on the lookout for *Psychic* magazine, published in San Francisco. When she was visiting a friend, she spied *Psychic* on the coffee table—a past issue, worn, and nearly a year old. Thumbing through it, curious about her mother's interest, she came across the only article I had written for the magazine in the six years it was published, on psychotherapy and meditation in the treatment of cancer, which was about Dr. Carl Simonton's work, with my picture and biographical sketch at the end. This unexpected encounter with me in the magazine led her to call the next day, a time when I had an opening. If she had called when she had first gotten my name, I probably would have referred her to someone else, as I had not had time available for a new patient for some time.

Both of these patients experienced meeting me as a meaningful coincidence. They had a sense of having had special circumstances arranged for us to work together, which gave them a conviction that our work would be significant from the beginning. Synchronicity conveyed a meant-to-be feeling. It took me much longer to appreciate that these meetings would be especially meaningful for me as well and that they would be significant for my own growth.

My work with the priest eventually became the case I wrote up in detail and presented to the certifying board as part of the final "rite of passage" to become a Jungian analyst. His analysis was full of synchronistic events, which strongly influenced the development of my thinking in this direction. It is a result in part of my experience with him that I now find myself writing this book on synchronicity.

The artist who felt fate had played a hand in leading her to me had a profound effect on my awareness of the nature of analysis. When, in the middle of this particular analysis, I unexpectedly found that I couldn't see my own way clearly, I reached a deeper understanding of alchemy as a metaphor for the process—and why Jung may have delved so deeply into the subject (in *Psychology and Alchemy;* in *Psychology of the Transference,* which uses an alchemical treatise as a means of explanation; and in *Mysterium Coniunctionis*). The analysis with her began to feel like being in a labyrinth or darkened maze together. In mythology, when Theseus goes into the labyrinth to confront the Minotaur, he has the aid of Ariadne's golden thread to lead him out. For me, as each new twist and bend of the psychological maze required a choice of action or interpretation, it seemed that intuition was the golden thread that had to be trusted to lead us out. I had to draw on something deeper than what I knew from my training and prior clinical experience, and through this experience I gained humility and the trust that I could count on receiving direction from dreams and synchronistic events.

Since analysis is a very intense human encounter, not just the patient is affected by the process: The power in the relationship to bring about change can affect the therapist as well. For this reason, Jung considered the analytic process similar to an alchemical reaction—for one element to be changed in the process (the patient), the other would also have to be affected (the analyst). As an analyst, it seems to me that my patients come through my office door bringing with them the opportunity and necessity for encountering aspects of myself. Whatever I need to become more conscious of, whatever could be an Achilles heel, whatever is my growing edge, synchronistically seems to arrive on my doorstep. Realizing this, when synchronicity seems to be playing a hand in bringing someone to me, I now wonder whether it will be a meeting of special significance for me as well as for the patient.

All people whose work involves helping others or teaching others would do well to keep synchronicity in mind. This matchmaker will probably bring significant others into their lives, creating opportunities for mutual growth or stirring up intense and troublesome feelings. In all synchronistic meetings, an important psychological element is active in one or both persons, lending an emotional charge to the situation. Attraction, aversion, or fascination are invariably present between the two people who meet through synchronistic means. This is because the meeting has brought an emotionally charged image or archetype up from the depths of the psyche and made it come alive. An intense emotional reaction to an archetypal image is quite natural.

We all have within us these powerful images, more varied than those provided by our parents, that reside in the collective unconscious, to which we all have access. When the Roman poet Terence said *"Nothing human is foreign to me,"* he was speaking as a person who is in touch with the collective unconscious and its myriad of archetypes, common to all human beings.

Archetypal images are multiple and varied; for example, the Patriarch or Father (Jehovah, Zeus), the Hero (Hercules, and, for some, John F. Kennedy), the Earth Mother (Demeter, maybe Golda Meir), the Beautiful Feminine (Helen of Troy, or Aphrodite), or Christ (Osiris), to name just a few. The ancient Greek gods and goddesses no longer live on Mount Olympus, but they are still alive and well, by whatever names we might call them, in our collective unconscious.

Once this archetypal layer is activated by a psychological situation that touches or evokes a particular archetype, then intense feelings are generated. For example, if Christ is the activated archetype, then several feeling responses are possible, depending on how this mixture of feeling and image is experienced. If it is evoked by a charismatic religious leader, then the archetype might be projected onto him, leading people to worship him devotedly (as if he were Christ). Or the archetype could be experienced inwardly—for one person it might be felt as an intense personal conviction that Christ lives within him or her, while another might be "possessed" by the archetype or totally identified with it, and so proclaim to the world "I am Christ."

When, in everyday life, a person "falls head over heels in

love," the loved one has provided the "hook" that attracts the archetypal projection. Often the hook is an esthetic quality, a particular physical characteristic, or personality style. Puzzled by the worshipful intensity, a friend may wonder, "What does he see in her?" aware that his friend is "seeing" something that he is not appreciating. What is seen is an archetypal image that is a projection; put another way, "Beauty is in the archetype of the beholder."

Negative images also carry the same larger-than-life qualities. A critical, grouchy boss may take on the dimensions of a vengeful Jehovah of the Old Testament. A selfish, intrusive older woman may seem to be a devouring being, like an aspect of Kali, the Hindu goddess of generation and destruction, to be appeased and feared. When a person evokes an emotion such as infatuation, fear, or exaggerated anger, something about that person's manner, some characteristic of his or hers, may hook an archetypal image. That person is then reacted to emotionally as if he or she were one and the same as the image. Everyone has done this, later to realize that "I overreacted" or "I discovered my idol had clay feet" or "I must have been enchanted" when the real human dimension reappears after the initial emotional reaction to the archetype.

What is outside of me, is in me: whenever a person is either magnetically drawn to someone who carries a positive archetype or overly condemns someone who is intensely felt to be a completely negative person, an archetype probably has been activated in the environment. Thus, what is being experienced "outside" is really an inner situation. Recall my sychronistic meeting with the priest: In his conscious experience, he was not aware that a woman can be trustworthy and caring. However, a positively regarded, supportive woman potentially existed on the archetypal level and had been imagined to exist in the form of a Japanese woman. When I appeared, fitting the archetype, this positive archetypal image was projected whole onto me. His immediate feelings of ease were not initially feelings toward me but feelings toward the image in his mind. The trust he had at this point was not based on knowing me but on his experience of me *as if* I were this positive feminine image.

His depression and feelings of worthlessness were related to an inner negative attitude; in his psyche was a powerful inner "bitch" who was depreciating him, telling him cuttingly and sarcastically how insignificant he was, how he deserved to feel bad, how meaningless and futile his efforts were. (I am reminded of a Jules Feiffer cartoon brought to me by another patient, of a man cringing as a hooded accuser hurls similar statements at him. The man then begins to stand up and fight back, finally repudiating the accuser; at which point the figure removes the hood and says "How can you say such things to your mother?") This man very much needed an inner relationship with the positive feminine, "who" if he were feeling rejected or discouraged would not take it as an opportunity to attack, unleashing hostile putdowns, but "who" could be encouraging and supportive. Until this capacity for self-nurture became part of his *inner* life, he could project it onto me, and I could temporarily carry it. He could then experience me as an encouraging, nurturing woman in his *outer* life (thanks initially to the Japanese woman image). Gradually, this positive attitude would become an inner figure or attitude, available to him when he was discouraged. The inner figure was the one he needed to meet when he encountered me in my waiting room.

It moves me to appreciate the fact that he sought therapy not knowing what he needed and immediately met "the archetype" he needed to meet. It was evoked in him at the moment of our meeting, and with time he became inwardly acquainted with it as well. Both the precisely tailored-to-fit outer psychiatrist and the important inner archetype were met synchronistically and simultaneously.

Some people have synchronistic meetings in which the same personality types or representatives of archetypal figures reappear again and again. Each time they bring that symbolic person onto "the stage" to reenact the same drama yet again. With one man, the repeated drama took the form of unpleasant interactions with what we came to refer to as "dragon ladies." He was the recipient of unwanted solicitous attentions from a certain type of older woman, who was saccharinely sweet on the surface, yet demanding, and toward whom he felt resentfully compliant. He experienced these women as devouring and powerful, and he resisted them in passive ways. He needed to discover and develop his own power, to feel the assertiveness and courage of the inner hero (to be a St. George). Also, he did distort the images of these women through his resentment and feelings of powerlessness. Although they were not really as monstrous as he experienced them, they did present a social face of sweetness that was not in harmony with the inner dissatisfaction and anger that they felt.

As he became inwardly stronger, he changed the nature of his pattern of interacting with this kind of woman. His apparently compliant, yet passively resistant style had encouraged them to increase their expectations and then to be more demanding and angry as he retreated. Now he was clear and firm from the beginning. Obviously his psychological growth would mean that he would have less trouble with this kind of woman. But there is no objective reason why there would be fewer such women for him to encounter, yet that did seem to be the case, even taking into consideration that such meetings would now be much less difficult. Because he had learned to spot such women, as part of his insight into what was happening, he now marveled at the change. Where previously they had confronted him everywhere, he now realized that there had been no new dragon ladies on any horizon in months.

Appreciating that "another version of that symbolic person is making an appearance again" helps. Recognizing the pattern is the beginning of wisdom, because it allows one to observe instead of being drawn, willy-nilly, toward the emotionally charged person. Every synchronistic meeting seems to involve archetypes of the collective unconscious in some way; hence the unconscious magnetism present as one is drawn toward an archetypal image. If the image is positive, some magic seems to surround the person. But if it is a negative archetype, several responses might occur—a cowering intimidation toward a larger-than-life power attributed to the person, or intense, inappropriate fear or hatred.

Many people seem to encounter a certain type of person every time they turn around, and thus their experiences seem to substantiate their assumptions. For example, if a man believes that all women are promiscuous, chances are that the "evidence" keeps piling up. The reasons are multiple and complex: Acting on his assumption, such a man will treat every woman he is involved with or marries with mistrust, assuming that she is or will be unfaithful. The emotional distance this creates, along with the resentment felt by the woman at being presumed guilty, increases the likelihood that she may turn to someone else for warmth and validation. By cause and effect, the presumed situation might then come about. Such a man might also be drawn to women whose personalities make promiscuity likely, in order to compulsively and neurotically repeat the situation. Again, cause and effect. Or perhaps the man projects the assumption onto a woman he perceives indistinctly. This is like a strong technicolor image from a movie projector falling on a person who is otherwise in the dark; what the man sees is his own projection, regardless of the characteristics of the individual woman. Finally, the projection may have a Pygmalion-like effect on an immature woman, in some way influencing her to take on the predetermined role.

Given the possibility of synchronicity—which is a hypothesis I add to the psychologically causal situations just described, this man might run into a promiscuous woman every time he turns around, not only because that's what he is prepared to see but because coincidentally that's who is really there. Synchronicity suggests that the outer world really does reflect the inner world, not just that it seems to. I might add that a Jungian perspective on this man's inner psyche would describe him as having a negative feminine aspect, which would affect him in two ways: It would color his view of women negatively, as already described, and his own "inner feminine" would probably be as defective as the image of women that he carried. Consequently, he probably would not have developed nurturing, loving, and relationship-oriented qualities and so quite possibly could not be trusted to be faithful himself.

If this man could accept the possibility that the world he experiences is a mirror and that what he sees and condemns is a reflection of what must change in himself, then change would be possible. For most people, altering the pattern of the way things are in the outer world is impossible, while changing what one sees as a problem in one's own psyche, although difficult, can be done.

Synchronicity provides yet another tool to help bring about individual change if a person can recognize a problem within by seeing the pattern reflected in the outer situation and then take responsibility for changing. Or as Richard Bach said in his book *Illusions,*

"Every person,
   All the events of your life
      Are there because you have drawn them there.
What you choose
   To do with them is
      Up to you.

A thirty-five-year-old woman once complained to me there were no eligible men, that every man she met was either gay, or turned out to take advantage of her, and was either unwilling or unable to maintain a commitment. Changing the focus from complaining about the lamentable quality of her social environment, to looking within herself, she discovered a couple of troublesome active archetypes. One was long suffering and maternal, an unappreciated Lady Bountiful who was always giving and forgiving, and who actually expected (and got) very little in return. Another (more surprising to her) find was a defiant (although inhibited in expression), angry (with a lid on) nonconformist, a closet adolescent in rebellion, who really did not want to settle down. She seemed to have a magnetic affinity for selfish, counterculture, boyish men whom she mothered and admired (her closet adolescent enjoyed his noncomformist actions vicariously).

As she saw the pattern and consequences of her interactions, she began to act differently. She reined in what she came to consider a misdirected maternal instinct and an adolescent lack of judgment and expressed her legitimate needs for caring and responsible behavior to the men in her life. The men in her life then started treating her better, a change that obviously was directly attributable to her changed expectations and behavior. Even more interesting, she now found herself meeting interesting, eligible, grown-up men who were coming out of the woodwork or wherever synchronicity found them. Which raises the question: Given synchronicity, when the woman is ready will the right man come?

Synchronistic meetings are like mirrors, reflecting back to us something of ourselves. In order to grow, we should take a good look. Synchronicity holds the promise that if we will change within, the patterns in our outer life will change also. If the people and events of our lives are here because we have drawn them here, then what happens in our lives apparently by chance or fortune is not really accidental.

CHAPTER 6

THE SYNCHRONISTIC WISDOM OF THE I CHING

*The I Ching as an oracle ·
Synchronicity as the underlying principle · The Tao as
basis for the philosophy and wisdom of the I Ching*

The *I Ching* or *Book of Changes* is a modern bestseller and an ancient book of philosophic wisdom. It is also an oracle in book form, consulted by many in the same spirit as those who once journeyed to Delphi to consult the oracle of Apollo. Some approach the book with reverence and feel they obtain wise and appropriate advice; others dismiss both it and the idea that it could work at all, as they consider oracles as being about as sensible as believing the message in a Chinese fortune cookie.

Synchronicity in life arises spontaneously, and through such events we realize that there is a linkage between ourselves and the world that we cannot account for by logical means. The *I Ching* reverses this sequence: We assume that synchronicity exists when we consult the *I Ching*. There is no rational explanation how it could possibly work; the method depends on synchronicity, and an uncannily correct reading provides emotional confirmation.

The *I Ching* is probably one of the most important books in the literature of the world, because the two branches of Chinese philosophy, Confucianism and Taoism, have common roots in the *I Ching*. It emphasizes eternal values in the middle of a continually changing universe, assumes a cosmos that has a discernible underlying pattern, and strongly advises holding to inner values yet counsels about action and attitudes appropriate to the outer situation. The *I Ching* teaches principles through which it may be possible to learn to live in harmony with the Tao, the invisible meaning-giving matrix of the universe.

I was introduced to the *I Ching* in 1967 by a patient during my first year in private practice. She had gone from a hopeless, immobilizing, black, suicidal depression into that gray, "blah" state that is an interface between deep depression and return to life with its many emotional colors. In this phase of recovery, she had a sense of going through the motions of life, once more functioning again, working effectively, seeing people, but the vitality and desire to be doing what she was doing had not yet returned.

She was discouraged and impatient, and there was a danger that she would give up or act destructively and impulsively because of these feelings. In this frame of mind, she had consulted the *I Ching* and came to my office to read what she had gotten. What followed was an eloquently descriptive metaphor about her situation. The reading was Hexagram 5, "Waiting (Nourishment)," which begins:

> All things have need of nourishment. But the gift of food comes in its own time, and for this one must wait. This hexagram shows the clouds in the heavens, giving rain to refresh all that grows . . . the rain will come in its own time. We cannot make it come; we have to wait for it. The idea of waiting is further suggested by the attributes of the two trigrams—strength within, danger in front. Strength in the face of danger does not plunge ahead but bides its time, whereas weakness in the face of danger grows agitated and has not the patience to wait.

The hexagram's focus on a need for nourishment as a way of describing her situation was fitting. I knew that there was no nourishment in what she was doing and that she found life a meaningless exercise. This stage of a depression is like land after a prolonged drought, waiting for the rain to come, the life-giving moisture that is needed to bring green life back to the wasteland. It is a disheartening and potentially danger-ous period, because there is enough energy to carry out an intent to commit suicide, should she despair that this period would never end.

The text offered her wise counseling on the attitude she needed to take during this difficult time:

> Waiting is not mere empty hoping. It has the inner certainty of reaching a goal. Such certainty alone gives that light which leads to success. This leads to the perseverance that leads to good fortune and bestows power to cross the great water.
>
> One is faced with a danger that must be overcome. Weak-ness and impatience can do nothing. Only a strong man can stand up to his fate, for his inner security enables him to endure to the end. This strength shows itself in uncompromising truth-fulness (with himself). It is only when we have the courage to face things exactly as they are, without any sort of self-decep-tion or illusion, that a light will develop out of events, by which the path to success may be recognized. This recognition must be followed by resolute and persevering action. For only the man who goes to meet his fate resolutely is equipped to deal with it adequately. Then he will be able to cross the great water —that is to say, he will be capable of making the necessary decision and of surmounting the danger.

This *I Ching* hexagram spoke directly to her and touched something within her. It supported a wavering part of her that was in a working alliance with me and strengthened it. Although it was her reading, I felt it also had meaning for me, as I needed to learn more patience, in order to allow people to recover and grow in their own time.

How does one consult the *I Ching*? Here is where syn-chronicity comes in, because the existence of synchronicity or an underlying Tao is the only basis on which it could work.

Logically there is no way to account for the accuracy and relevance of the readings obtained. Like the bumble bee, which according to aerodynamic theory, shouldn't be able to fly, the *I Ching* shouldn't work as an oracle, but does.

There are two main ways to make an *I Ching* reading. In either method, an individual seeking advice from the book must first formulate the question in words. He or she may then ritually divide forty-nine yarrow stalks six times in succession to obtain six numbers, corresponding to the six lines that form a hexagram. Or, using the shorter coin method, three coins are taken up and thrown down together a total of six times, each throw giving a line. Each hexagram refers the reader to a particular text. The Wilhelm-Baynes edition of the *I Ching* has a useful section in the appendix entitled "On Consulting the Oracle" describing how to do the yarrow stalk oracle and the coin oracle. A key at the end of the book lists all the hexagrams and directs the reader to the text which reveals the meaning of each.

Just as spontaneous synchronistic events resonate with and parallel active, emotionally laden inner situations, the *I Ching* works best when there is an inner situation of tension and intensity. It does not work as a parlor game. The *I Ching* answers questions when that question is emotionally a central focus. I usually frame the question by asking, "Comment on the nature of the situation and on the attitude and action I should follow at this time." Since the *I Ching* usually speaks to this anyway, I feel it might as well be asked directly. (If one asks the *I Ching* a frivolous question when one is emotionally involved in something else, it invariably "answers" the underlying situation, not the unimportant question.) Joseph Henderson, a distinguished Jungian analyst and scholar, sees the use of the *I Ching* as "a practical application of Taoism in everyday life" and advises that

> In asking their questions, people had better wait until they have reduced the question to its simplest, most specific form, and to be sure that they really cannot answer it themselves . . . then the nature of Taoist symbolism is truly respected, which might be described as seeking to provide a kind of illumi-

nation of the real in combination with an ongoing process of self-realization.

The *I Ching* itself, in Book II, called the Ta Chuan or Great Treatise, puts it this way:

> Therefore the superior man, whenever he has to make or do something, consults the Changes, and he does so in words. It takes up his communication like an echo; neither far nor near, neither dark nor deep exist for it, and thus he learns of the things of the future. If this book were not the most spiritual thing on earth, how could it do this?

Not all individuals are equally able to work with the *I Ching.* One needs a capacity for intuiting meaning and appreciating metaphor and image, as well as a philosophical outlook in sympathy with the idea of the Tao. The *I Ching* warns, *"If the person consulting the oracle is not in contact with the Tao, he does not receive an intelligible answer, since it would be of no avail."* In my office, I work with the *I Ching* when it is brought up by a person I am seeing. Like a spontaneous event or a dream, I feel it to be another expression of the activity of the symbolic psyche, which can provide us with a valuable insight into the meaning of the current situation. If a patient brings an *I Ching* reading into an analytic session, it was a significant event for that person. I work with it as I do dreams and synchronistic events. Even though the metaphoric images in the *I Ching* were not created in the psyche of the person, and so are less individual, I have found it helpful for understanding the situation to seek personal meanings in the images and symbols. Amplifications through association to the metaphors presented has been very helpful.

For example, an image in Hexagram 34, "The Power of the Great," *"A goat butts against a hedge, it cannot go backward, it cannot go forward."* This is a picture of a situation in which a person is caught fruitlessly expending energy in a useless, obstinate struggle. Further amplification revealed two additional insights. Fear of being thought of as "the goat" was one of the reasons for stubbornly continuing the effort. Also the tendency to exaggerate or overvalue monetary loss was associated with what this person called a negative "Capricorn" (the goat, astrologically) element in himself.

Another metaphor, from Hexagram 47, "Oppression," has this image:*"He is oppressed by creeping vines."* This describes bonds that can easily be broken. To the patient who got this reading, the image suggested "clinging vine" as a personal association, and the mixture of guilt and hostility that dependency evoked was the immobilizing psychological problem to be faced. By associating to the image, the patient gained much personal insight.

I find that sometimes weeks go by when no one brings up the *I Ching.* Some people bring it up once in a while; others in my practice have never heard of it, while yet others have been introduced to the *I Ching* but never found it personally significant. As with dreams and spontaneous synchronicity, great individual variation exists.

During the period while I was writing this chapter, two women in my practice brought up the same *I Ching* hexagram. Both were in marriages that had reached a crisis stage. Each considered separation and had thrown the coins for further insight that the *I Ching* might provide. Both got Hexagram 49, "Revolution (Molting)," which describes revolution as analogous to the molting of an animal's pelt in the course of a year. This analogy is then applied to the moltings in political life, the great revolutions connected with changes of governments. Although their marriage situations were quite different, these women had their roles in common: Both women were in revolt against the values held by their husbands and saw the need to change the governing principles of their marriages.

Once a woman I was seeing repeatedly got Hexagram 62, "Preponderance of the Small," over a two-year period. She would either get it by the throw of the coins, or would get another hexagram with a moving line and find the moving line changed it into "Preponderance of the Small." The repetition was exceedingly convincing, and she heeded the advice, which she did not always particularly welcome, because she did agree with the *I Ching*'s view of her situation even if she did not like to be reminded of it. Getting the same advice over and over impressed her. The hexagram has as the judgment:

> *Preponderance of the small. Success.*
> *Perseverance furthers.*
> *Small things may be done; great things should not be*
>   *done.*
> *The flying bird brings the message:*
> *It is not well to strive upward. It is well to remain below.*
> *Great good fortune.*

The colloquial message was "Keep on plugging, and don't get any big ideas." It advises being conscientious and thrifty, dutifully working at what she was doing, as this was not the time to attempt anything greater. In her life, she was working her way through college toward a graduate degree in counseling. The repetitive hexagram encouraged her to keep on a track she had set for herself, a career for which I felt she had a special aptitude, as well as personal experiences that made success likely.

This woman usually consulted the *I Ching* when another career possibility arose and appealed to her more impulsive qualities. Getting a moving line such as the following one discouraged the notion that there were short-cuts or easier ways of achieving her own goals:

> *Six at the beginning means:*
> *The bird meets with misfortune through flying.*

The discussion that followed elaborated further on the meaning:

> *"The bird ought to remain in the nest until it is fledged.*
> *If it tries to fly before this, it invites misfortune. We ought*
> *to put up with traditional ways as long as possible; other-*
> *wise we exhaust ourselves and our energy and still achieve*
> *nothing."*

To her, it seemed to advise that she stay with her education until she had credentials and experience.

The work of analysis, as I see it, does well to take the wisdom of the *I Ching* into account, the basic, Taoist philosophy behind the text that recognizes the need of the individual to be in relationship to the cyclic nature of the seasons; to be either active or inactive, depending on what is appropriate for the time, and therefore to be in harmony both with what one is and what the season is. The word "season" is used broadly here. One meaning refers to the "seasons of life"; for example, the independent young adult stage or the childbearing years, or the midlife period, or facing one's imminent death—each are different "seasons" requiring differing responses from us. Another "season" to be taken into account might be whether it is peacetime or wartime, a period of economic depression or of affluence. Or the "season" may be purely personal, a time of ease or a time of testing and hardship. In Ecclesiastes 3:1–2, there is a poetic litany that begins, *"For everything there is a season, and a time for every matter under heaven: a time to be born and a time to die; a time to plant, and a time to pluck up what is planted."* Like the *I Ching*, this passage emphasizes that there are seasons through which we must pass.

It would be folly to impatiently expect daffodils to push their green shoots up in midwinter just because one is tending the soil in which the bulbs are lying. People, like plants and trees, grow according to their own inner clock as well as in relationship to the outer seasons. It is important to respect the rhythms and seasons in each of our lives and to pay attention to dreams and synchronistic events that will help us to grow in an organic way.

Attunement to the situation is one value held in common by analysts and the *I Ching*. Also similar is an attitude that respects restraint, that takes action only when appropriate, and that emphasizes perseverence through periods of difficulty. The philosophy of the *I Ching* readily applies to my metaphor for analysis.

For me, doing analysis is analogous to gardening. The relationship between analyst and patient, with its rules of confidentiality, and its quality of sanctuary where it is safe to bring up anything, serves as a container for the process of growth.

Removing weeds and rocks, and tilling and watering the soil are preliminary tasks in gardening and are like the psychotherapy phase of analysis. The hindrances to growth, the weeds and rocks—whether in one's early family life or in one's current situation—need to be eliminated. Whatever has crowded out the individual's growth needs to be recognized and removed. Water, which is like feeling, must be brought to the situation in order to allow the defenses to soften and be penetrated. In this way, feelings from others can get through to provide nourishment, like water gets through to the roots of a plant that have been in parched, thick, clayey soil. In analysis, growth occurs underground or deep in the unconscious; later, it manifests itself in what shows above the ground.

What comes into being depends on the nature of the seed. A good gardener helps each plant to grow fully and produce whatever it was meant to: whether fruit or vegetable or flower, to be fully whatever it was meant to be—oak, redwood, geranium, or even cactus.

Often an analyst is a supporting pole for a period of time in another person's life. Most growing things become sturdy enough to eventually continue growing on their own, absorbing the water and sunshine of the environment, taking nourishment from the soil in which they are now deeply rooted, in a life of significant soil.

From what I have said about the *I Ching,* I obviously respect the philosophical richness, and the appropriateness of the advice given. Significantly, of course, in each example I have used the individual was in an emotionally significant time and used the *I Ching* as an additional consultant. I have also seen the *I Ching* used unwisely and promiscuously, used like a newspaper horoscope to decide whether to leave the house, for example, on the basis of omenlike words or phrases without due reflection or understanding the meaning of the hexagram itself. Such consultation defeats its purpose and merely stifles the growth and the development of the individual.

If this chapter has been your introduction to the *I Ching,* then I may have introduced you to a wise, contemplative, and helpful friend. In the concluding words of his foreword to the *I Ching,* Jung has this to say about getting acquainted with the *Book of Changes*:

The *I Ching* does not offer itself with proofs and results; it does not vaunt itself, nor is it easy to approach. Like a part of nature, it waits until it is discovered. It offers neither facts nor power, but for lovers of self-knowledge, or wisdom—if there be such—it seems to be the right book. To one person its spirit appears to be as clear as day; to another shadowy as twilight; to a third, dark as night. He who is not pleased by it does not have to find it true. Let it go further into the world for the benefit of those who can discern its meaning.

CHAPTER 7

PARAPSYCHOLOGICAL PIECES OF THE SYNCHRONICITY PUZZLE

Through participation in
Psychic *magazine, a firsthand look at parapsychology ·*
Mind over matter, ESP, and poltergeist phenomena ·
"Impossible" ESP tests and the archetype of the miracle ·
The symmetrical universe of quantum physics

In 1968, my husband and I, who were then visionary intuitives and babes in the business woods, decided that we would start a new magazine on psychic phenomena covering the emerging field of parapsychology, which Jim would edit and publish. Our dreamer selves envisioned the need for a high-quality publication that would report on the many facets of this new science as we entered the Age of Aquarius. The already established publications in this field emphasized the occult and did not do justice to the impressive research and writing of real significance.

Jim had had a long-time interest in psychic and philosophical matters, and he had considerable writing experience. As an account executive in a growing and successful public relations firm, he had become increasingly disheartened at having to write about people and institutions that he did not support. The clients he represented were corporations interested in shaping their public images and in getting their way. The skyline of San Francisco was becoming Manhattanized in the late 1960s by such companies, and his latest and largest client was interested in filling more of the San Francisco Bay with a multimillion dollar complex. He did not like the idea of being professionally engaged in helping this to happen, while personally valuing the environment. The decision to begin a magazine came out of this mixture of vision and dissatisfaction.

Psychic Magazine began as a "Mom and Pop business," with one full-time employee. Everything else was freelanced or done by Jim, who wrote, edited, and managed production and business. I helped where I could, at the very beginning even logging subscriptions on Saturdays, occasionally reading manuscripts, sharing in decisions, and meeting with researchers, authors, or potential investors. But mainly I continued in my own profession of psychiatry while Jim devoted full time to the magazine. Given all the effort, energy, and care the magazine took, we used to refer to it somewhat jokingly as "our first child."

During the eight years *Psychic* was published, it became the popular and respected authority in the field and helped to give national recognition to psychic individuals and organizations, reporting on the findings of parapsychological researchers, and discussing the implications of such research. It was, throughout, a beautiful magazine, with color and quality. Then in early 1977, David Hammond, who had been a vital participant for four years, became a partner in the enterprise. Also, *Psychic* became *New Realities* at that time, as the old title no longer reflected the direction the magazine was taking. As well as establishing the authenticity and breadth of parapsychological events and research, it now began to feature articles exploring the relevance of parapsychology to the individual. The magazine broadened into spiritual and psychic consciousness, holistic health, environment, lifestyles, and other new ways of thinking and being.

Although my main professional interests were in psychiatry and Jungian analysis, during the years in which Jim published *Psychic* I continued to meet significant people in the field and kept abreast of the research and of individuals with special talents. As a Jungian analyst, I found it unnecessary to compartmentalize the two fields of psychology and parapsychology, because Jung's concept of synchronicity included parapsychological phenomena and so was not in conflict. In contrast, most of mainstream psychology has been antagonistic or indifferent to parapsychology.

In 1972 I went to Durham, North Carolina, to interview J. B. Rhine for *Psychic* Magazine. As I set off, I felt as though I were going back into time, to talk with a famous historical personality. Dr. Joseph Banks Rhine is the "father of parapsychology" in this country, responsible for the classical laboratory work and breakthrough that statistically proved the existence of extrasensory perception and psychokinesis, or mind over matter. Rhine was the embattled pioneer who struggled to bring respectability and acceptance to the field within the scientific community. His position was similar to Freud's and Jung's in psychology. As a founding father for a new field, he attracted the men and women who would be the next several generations of researchers. He and his wife Dr. Louisa E. Rhine had spent over fifty years trail-blazing and then doing the hard, repetitious work of establishing the scientific foundation for parapsychology. Rhine became a household word in the center of a scientific storm after publishing a monograph entitled *Extra-Sensory Perception* in 1934, before I was born.

I met Dr. Rhine and his wife across the street from Duke University, at the Foundation for Research on the Nature of Man, which they had established in 1962. On a quiet tree-lined street, in what had been an older, gracious house, the newest parapsychological research was still going on, now using computers and random number generators, as well as other complex machinery for testing. Dr. Rhine, born in 1895, was then in his late seventies. I found him to be a tall, straight-standing, craggy-faced, handsome man with white hair, younger in all ways than his age. Given the dry, statistical quality of his research, I had not expected him to be the warm, expressive, and charming man that he was. The Rhines had been biologists who initially entered the field intent on inquiring into the survival of consciousness after death, which led them to studying mediums, and from there into investigating "the very means by which a medium could be a medium." They began concentrating first on clairvoyance and telepathy, then on precognition, and later on psychokinesis.

Modern parapsychology began with the Rhines, who with their students, collaborators, and now their colleagues in university settings throughout the country brought psychic phenomena into the laboratory. Rigorous, repetitive tests were run under scientific controls in order to produce statistically valid results. The field lost its aura of mysticism and became dull reading as scientific jargon and statistical tables replaced the fascinating anecdotal cases. Both the spiritual and occult nuances were shed in the process of gaining reputability. The idea of the laboratory data being a result of fraud or conspiracy (which disbelievers clung to as being more plausible than ESP) became ridiculous as the number and stature of investigators to join the Rhines grew by leaps and bounds.

Final respectability was granted to parapsychology by the scientific establishment in 1969, when the prestigious American Association for the Advancement of Science accepted the Parapsychological Association as a member organization. This, after two previous applications had been rejected, with Margaret Mead nominating, was a sign of a change in attitude toward this field.

While the scientists in the psychic field were impressive, many of the psychic individuals themselves were decidedly disappointing to me. Even though other people swore by the accuracy of their psychic readings, I remained unimpressed, because efforts to "read me" were inaccurate or far too general. Early in 1973, I began to realize that I might be the limiting factor—that my initial skepticism, followed by the mixture of disparagement and disappointment I felt inwardly when they failed to impress me, might be contributing to their poor performance. It seemed likely, given the encouraging emotional setting of rapport where telepathy usually occurs spontaneously, that my attitude might be the block, that I was limiting the experience. I read John Lilly's autobiography, *Center of the Cyclone,* and was struck by one of his ideas, which I paraphrase thus: *We must transcend our own limiting beliefs in order to grow beyond them, or in order to have the experiences which allow us to grow.*

This is what occurs in psychotherapy. People seek therapy because something is not working well in their lives, when their efforts to find answers or solutions or to change things for the better have not succeeded. In this defeated frame of mind, their "set" view of themselves or their situation is not immutably fixed and is open to change. Often people have been programmed by overly critical or rejecting parents to accept a limited or negative view of themselves or to be suspicious or mistrustful of others. The therapy situation allows old beliefs to be examined and held in suspension, while new ways of perceiving oneself or others and acting in the world are tried. In order to grow, *the mental limits are the handicaps that must be transcended.*

Given this understanding, it seemed to me that I had to suspend my challenging, critical, "go ahead and show me" attitude. Instead, I needed to meet a psychic individual when I was feeling receptive and hopeful that he or she would be successful. I determined to try this new attitude at the next opportune moment, deciding I would be present whenever Jim next did an interview with a psychic.

The next interview subject, of whom I had not known at that point, was Uri Geller. Synchronistically, the opportunity to meet the most impressive psychic individual of that time occurred immediately after I had changed an inner attitude. Geller, an intense, good-looking, young Israeli, could consciously affect objects with his mind, as well as telepathically and clairvoyantly receive impressions.

Jim interviewed him in a San Francisco Holiday Inn hotel room. Two scientists from Stanford Research Institute were present, as well as most of the magazine staff. In order to demonstrate psychokinesis (PK), or mind over matter, Uri offered to try to bend the hotel room's Schlage brass key by lightly stroking the metal and willing it to bend. As we watched, it did bend! Then Jim placed it on a piece of paper and outlined the angle of the bend. It lay on the coffee table, untouched by Geller or anyone else, observed by us all. And when we next checked it, the angle of the bend was more acute—the metal key had continued to bend.

Geller demonstrated what parapsychologists had established statistically in laboratory settings—that mind can influence matter (by some as yet unknown means). For me, it was a meaningful coincidence to have an opportunity for this eye-witness experience as soon as I had laid aside my skepticism. It was another one of those experiences that make me believe the principle that "When a pupil is ready, the teacher will come." The readiness is a change in an inner attitude, and then, "coincidentally," a parallel outer event occurs.

When Geller tries to bend a key or fix a broken watch by mentally concentrating on it, or a lucky-streak gambler at Las Vegas feels "hot" and can "call the dice," or when a laboratory subject tries to influence whatever the test object may be—from a machine that throws dice to a magnetometer that measures gravitational fields—all are *consciously* trying to demonstrate mind over matter, or psychokinesis.

The *unconscious* influence of mind over matter is also an interesting situation. This is where the poltergeist phenomenon comes in. A popular subject for the newspaper reporter, poltergeists are associated with strange, unexplainable goings-on in a house: Objects move on their own, flying through the air or behaving in other even more bizarre ways. In parapsychology circles, this is referred to by the more scientific designation of "recurrent spontaneous psychokinesis." The word "poltergeist" was derived from the German word for "mischievous ghost," because such houses seemed haunted by prank-playing spooks. The serious study of such matters is, appropriately, a German research concern. Psychiatrist Hans Bender, Germany's foremost parapsychologist and his investigative research team at the Institute for Border Areas of Psychology and Mental Health of Freiburg University, at the edge of the Black Forest, are responsible for some of the best-documented cases. Mind-boggling and far-

out events were found to have occurred—objects that penetrated walls, locked cupboards, and boxes. In the investigative studies, objects were apparently teleported and electrical circuitry disrupted, as well as the more usual situation of
things flying through the air. Bender has found that almost
always there is an adolescent in considerable inner turmoil
in the "spooked" house. Alan Vaughan, a former editor of
Psychic who spent some time with Bender, reported,

> *Agreeing with the theories of the famous Swiss psycholo-
> gist, Carl Gustav Jung, Bender argues that psyche and
> matter seem 'inseparably entangled, and that inner psy-
> chological states and external physical events can become
> fused by powerful emotional and psychic energies' and
> with a few rare adolescents, this fusion results in polter-
> geist phenomena.*

Poltergeist movement, disruption, and breakage manifested
in the outer world is a form of synchronicity in which the
outer situation seems to express the conflict, repression, and
confusion of the inner world of that adolescent. (I have won-
dered whether the particular objects that fly through the air,
materialize in another room, tip over, fall, and break and the
electrical disruptions have a symbolic meaning for the specific adolescent. Not being on an investigatory path, it is a
speculation which I hope someone will look into one day.)

Instances in which the physical world seems to be affected,
influenced, or reacting to the human mind imply a demon-
strable connection between our minds or emotions and the
physical universe. The Eastern mystic says that this is the
Tao. Jung called it the *collective unconscious* and *synchronicity.*

Another area that concerns parapsychology is extrasensory
perception or ESP, which includes *telepathy,* or direct mind
to mind communication; *clairvoyance,* or the ability to "see"
or "know" of an event occurring out of the range of ordinary
senses; and *precognition,* or knowing what will occur in the
future. In postulating synchronicity, Jung included all of
these as examples of meaningful coincidence between person and event in which an emotional or symbolic connection

cannot be explained by cause and effect.

In situations in which ESP occurs spontaneously and knowledge is received consciously, there is usually an emotional link. Even in impersonal laboratory-controlled guessing experiments, the element of emotion is critical—in this case, emotional involvement in the experiment. Rhine found that there was always a decline effect in good ESP subjects: At the beginning, when there was high interest, the result was significantly better than later, when boredom or disinterest at the repetitious nature of the experiments set in.

Dr. Gertrude Schmeidler, a professor at City College in New York, began investigating ESP while a research associate at Harvard University. Her first experiment is now an historical classic. She separated people by their attitudes toward ESP: the "sheep" who believed in ESP, the "goats" who disbelieved. She found that the believers scored consistently higher than the disbelievers, who scored below chance.

In Schmeidler's and Rhine's experiments, the subject has an impossible task as far as the conscious ego is concerned. Imagine the situation: You are asked to make a sequential choice of symbols, trying to match them to an already determined list that is unavailable to you. Or, in case this isn't difficult enough, try another test: Again make a sequential choice of symbols and try to match them to a list that will be chosen in the future and does not even exist as of that moment. Such tasks raise the questions: "How is one to know? How can one do the impossible?"

Optimistically, "sheep" enter into the task with the belief that ESP is possible even in such circumstances, and they approach the task with hope. The "goats," however, the disbelievers, find their skepticism further bolstered by the "impossibility of the task."

Jung, on manuscript notes addressed to Ira Progoff, compared the ESP situation to myths where the hero faces an impossible situation:

> The test person either doubts the possibility of knowing something one cannot know, or hopes that it will be possible and that the miracle will happen. At all events, the test person

being confronted with a seemingly impossible task finds himself in the archetypal situation, which so often occurs in myths and fairy tales, where divine intervention, i.e., a miracle, offers the only solution.

By approaching this impossible ESP task with hopeful expectancy and mental intensity, a person evokes what Jung called "the archetype of the miracle" or the archetype of "magic effect." In this state of expectancy, the "miracle" can occur; then ESP results are highly positive.

Prayer evokes the same psychological state of hopeful expectancy. The person who sincerely approaches the *I Ching* needing an answer or some direction about something about which he or she is highly concerned and focused, hoping for some help to resolve a decision, also is in a similar state of focused expectancy. In this state, the *I Ching* reading that results is likely to be highly relevant. Being in such a state of mind before bedtime and mentally requesting a dream that might help also often produces dreams that can provide symbolic answers to seemingly unresolvable psychological situations. In every one of these situations, the person has conceded that the personal ego cannot provide an answer— either because, as with ESP, it is beyond the ego's capacity or function to do so, or because the ego is conflicted and cannot decide what to do; the person seeks further direction from beyond the ego, having appreciated the impasse the ego is in.

The hopeful expectancy that there is "something" beyond the ego is based on that individual's or humanity's experience of "something" greater than itself. This is the experience of the collective unconscious or of the power of the archetypal level, in which that "something greater" is directly experienced in an intuitively felt way: One then "knows" the answer, or "knows" God, or experiences the Tao.

To receive the experience, the person must be receptive. Consciously entering a state of hopeful expectancy is one way in which the archetypal layer of the collective unconscious is constellated. This may be one of the meanings behind the biblical statement from Matthew 7:7 *"Ask*

*and it will be given to you, seek and you will find, knock
and it will be opened to you."* In fairytales and myths, a
hero or heroine goes on a difficult quest in a hopeful state of
mind. With courage, perseverance, and often naivete or in-
nocence, he or she encounters an impossible situation and
finds unexpected help or magical intervention occurring at
crucial moments.

Our journey through life may follow such a pattern. If we
live with a hopeful assumption that what we do with our lives
is important and has meaning, and if we act accordingly with
integrity, hope, courage, and compassion, then "divine intervention" provides answers when we face difficulties. "Divine
intervention" can take many forms and can mean that access
to the collective unconscious is invoked by our conscious
attitude. A creative solution may emerge from within our
minds, or an amazing synchronicity may occur that solves the
situation, or a dream may provide direction or the answer
may come in meditation (all forms of "divine intervention").
Depending on the metaphor for this process, an individual
may experience this "divine intervention" either within a
religious context or totally without religious reference. When
this happens, the person is having an archetypal experience,
along with the intuitive insight, creative solution, synchronistic event, or experience of God. Usually he or she also has a
sense of grace or a feeling of joy.

Joy is the emotion that the artist, theoretician, or inventor
experiences at the moment of creation. Joy accompanies anything transcendent—in which the ego experiences something greater than itself. Joy is a mood whenever something
"new" is brought into being. It is present with a heightened
awareness of actualizing one's potentialities and always accompanies an intuitively felt Tao experience. However,
when evidence is gathered to prove something scientifically,
joy is not the prevailing mood. Instead, satisfaction or gratifi-
cation is felt as evidence mounts to validate a position. This
is so even when that research seems to point to a conception
of reality that is remarkably like the mystical concept of the
Tao.

Research into precognition seems to support the possibility

that time is eternally present and that linear time is an illusion; although we usually experience living only in the present, precognition implies that present and future may exist simultaneously. Research in telepathy so far shows no decreasing ability over distance, so that space as we measure it is discounted as a barrier. Clairvoyance and telepathy continue to operate while subjects are placed in lead-lined Faraday boxes, suggesting that such consciousness does not depend on electromagnetic energy or any known "causal" means of transmission. If matter can interpenetrate other matter, as reported in investigations into poltergeist phenomena, and if mind can influence matter, as in psychokinesis experiments, than all the usual physical laws governing matter, energy, and time do not seem to apply.

The only consistent factor found in ESP and PK so far is the psychological element. The declining success rate in tests seems to be a function of emotional involvement. Spontaneous telepathy or clairvoyance involve people with other people or situations that emotionally concern them. Poltergeist phenomena or runs of luck with dice seem related to altered psychological states. Since the emotional involvement of the person is the necessary factor or the common denominator in all ESP and PK events, they all fall under the category of synchronicity—in which there is a connection between an event or situation and an involved person who finds it meaningful.

Each bit of parapsychological research or new psychic event provides another piece in a vast synchronicity puzzle, although it is still a very incomplete picture, in which most of the pieces seem to be missing. We lack even the boundary edges. Yet what we do have in parapsychology is significant, because it links the subjective element of mind and emotions to the physical universe and proves that some unseen connection or unknown energy within us links us to others and to far-off events and influences matter.

Theoretical physics adds to this scientific picture. When the eminently respectable "hard" science of physics entered the theoretical world of subatomic physics, where quantum theory and relativity were proven by experiments, Nobel prize winners right and left described a reality that sounded increasingly like the Eastern idea of the Tao. Physicist Fritjof Capra brought the two concepts of theoretical physics and Eastern mysticism together in his book *The Tao of Physics.* Arthur Koestler, in *The Roots of Coincidence,* and Capra describe the emergence of a wholly nonmaterial world, in which there is no such stuff as matter, where things we normally see or touch consist of patterns of energy that are forever moving and changing, where there are particles that can turn into waves that can travel backward in time, and where everything is part of a dance that continually moves, where space and time are aspects of a continuum and an underlying pattern of oneness seems to exist.

My one foray into physics was a short-lived excursion toward this vision of a patterned universe. Taking a course in premedical physics one summer at the University of California, I was inspired by teaching assistants who were graduate students in physics working "up on the hill" at the Cyclotron (which is situated above the Berkeley campus). They had felt in a small way, "in on" recent discoveries of the antiproton, which was sought because "it had to exist—because the universe was symmetrical." My imagination was stirred by the idea that perfect balance existed—that each atomic particle had its matched opposite was beautiful and awesome to me. I think the intuitive feeling I had on looking up at the stars, in some way was paralleled by the concept of symmetry underlying theoretical physics; both had to do with a sense of a patterned, moving, meaningful universe, of which I was a part. Now, according to Arthur Koestler,

> Since the discovery of the first small "anti" particle, the antielectron, physicists have found—or produced in their laboratories—antiparticles corresponding to every known particle. The fifty particles known today and their fifty "antis" are in every respect alike, except that they have opposite electric charges, magnetic moments, and opposite "spin" and "strangeness."

The concept of a symmetrical universe was the first time that an idea, rather than a feeling, deeply touched me.

With this vision as an inspiration, I signed up for calculus and engineering physics—only to drop them when my intuition ran head on into my lack of knack for this sort of thing. But this one glimpse, which was yet another way of appreciating the vision of the Tao, has remained with me.

Wolfgang Pauli, who developed one of the key concepts of modern physics—the Pauli exclusion principle, a principle of mathematical symmetry—thought that parapsychological phenomena including apparent coincidences were the visible traces of an underlying, untraceable principle in the universe. Arthur Koestler felt that this provided the basis for Pauli's collaboration with Jung, in which "Jung used Pauli, so to speak, as a tutor in modern physics." This collaboration produced two publications. Pauli wrote an essay called *The Influence of Archetypal Ideas on the Scientific Theories of Kepler,* a study on the emergence of science from mysticism as exemplified by Johannes Kepler, a mystic and the founder of modern astronomy. Jung's work was called *Synchronicity: An Acausal Connecting Principle.* Their joint publications symbolically joined physics and psychology. This was Jung's definitive statement about synchronicity, in which he postulated that synchronicity was a principle as important as causality and in which he brought the concept into psychology.

With the idea of synchronicity, psychology joined hands with parapsychology and theoretical physics in seeing an underlying "something" akin to what the mystic has been seeing all along. The important element that synchronicity adds is a dimension of personal meaning that acknowledges what a person intuitively feels when a synchronistic event is directly experienced. Theories and laboratory experiences make thinkable the idea of an underlying invisible connection between everything in the universe. But when it is an intuitively felt experience, a *spiritual* element enters. The human psyche may be the one receiver in the universe that can correctly apprehend the meaning underlying everything, the meaning that has been called the Tao or God.

These are only hints and guesses,
Hints followed by guesses; and the rest
Is prayer, observance, discipline, thought and action.
                    The Four Quartets: The Dry Salvages
                                        T. S. Eliot

CHAPTER 8

THE TAO AS PATH WITH HEART

The **tao** *as a way to live in har-*
mony with the eternal **Tao** · *The path with heart* · *In-*
tuitive feeling as guide · *The inner journey to the East*

The heart has its reasons
Which reason does not understand.

Blaise Pascal

n ancient China, there was a
distinction between the
metaphysical, spiritual **Tao** of the Taoist philosophers, the
eternal, Great Tao, and the **tao** of Confucianism, an ethical
ideal of balance between the development of one's inner
wisdom and evidence of it in outer activity. "Sageliness
within and kingliness without" was the goal of psychological
development. Sageliness was an inner achievement; kingliness was the evidence of this in the outer life. The king as
symbol was "mediator between heaven and earth," "a virtu-
ous, whole, and balanced person." The two meanings of **Tao**
and **tao** are not in conflict. They supplement and reinforce
each other, because **tao** addresses itself to how a person who
experiences the eternal **Tao** may live his or her life.

Assuming that an underlying **Tao** connects everything in a given moment, Chinese people consulted the *I Ching* for advice on the action or attitude that was appropriate in following the **tao.**

Since an *I Ching* hexagram is arrived at by dividing yarrow stalks or throwing coins and by then looking at the corresponding reading, synchronicity would have to be operating for a meaningful coincidence to arise between the reading and the situation. The advice found in the *I Ching*—much of which was elaborated on by Confucius and his followers in the commentaries—is directed toward the ideal of basing outer action on inner wisdom.

The Great **Tao** then, is the underlying premise on which the *I Ching* works, and synchronicity is the manifestation of the Great Tao. The ethical ideal of there being a **tao** or "way to live" in harmony with the Great **Tao** is the philosophical base.

To understand **tao,** it helps to examine the components of the Chinese pictograph character. Mai-Mai Sze, author of *The Tao of Painting* described the pictograph for **tao**—which translates into "path, road, or way"—as being made up of two elements, *ch'o* and *shou.* *Ch'o* is a complex configuration composed of "a left foot taking a step," combined with another symbol meaning "to halt." *Shou* means "head," which suggests the idea that thought is involved. The connotations of the pictograph are that a step-by-step progression is involved, in which pauses are taken, to think before making the next step. Furthermore, the left foot as a yin direction would imply that the **tao** is an inner path.

Since the Chinese character for **tao** was a combination of a head and foot, it also symbolizes the idea of wholeness, which by implication requires spiritual growth. Thus **tao** can be appreciated as an inner way toward head-to-foot harmony. Furthermore, the "head" symbol was associated with heaven, the sun, and masculine yang energy, while the foot was equated with the earth and feminine yin energy. This path, or **tao,** then must also be an integration of the two forces, heaven and earth, masculine and feminine, yin and yang. The Chinese character or pictograph for **tao** clearly refers to an inner spiritual path to be consciously followed.

The Eternal **Tao** also carries the meaning of path as a way to live, to travel through life with a conscious awareness of being part of a divinely existing universe. It is a way of being, a **tao** that acknowledges the **Tao**.

In journeying through life, what is evident to others is the outer path taken. Direction, partner, and lifestyle can be seen. The inner path is much less evident to the eye. As we travel on our paths, we may be venturing into new territory, trail-blazing as we go, or we may be on a broad highway, well traveled and well worn. We can follow the crowd, pushed and pulled along by others, or we can, even in the midst of a crowd, be consciously making our own way, pausing to consider and listening to an inner drummer.

Which way to go? What to listen to? What signs to follow? There are so many potentially confusing directions, so much clutter and clamor around us, that drown out our capacity to stay aware of the "still point" as we travel on whatever path we choose. Perhaps, the outer paths "lead nowhere," the significance being whether we are in touch with an inner path as we travel on any of the many outer paths.

In *The Teachings of Don Juan,* Carlos Castaneda focused on the question of which path to follow and how to make the choice. Don Juan's advice to Castaneda was as follows:

> Anything is one of a million paths. Therefore you must always keep in mind that a path is only a path: If you feel you should not follow it, you must not stay with it under any conditions. To have such clarity you must lead a disciplined life. Only then will you know that any path is only a path, and there is no affront, to oneself or to others, in dropping it if that is what your heart tells you to do. But your decision to keep on the path or leave it must be free of fear or ambition . . . look at every path closely and deliberately. Try it as many times as you think necessary.

Don Juan emphasized the need to consciously decide which path to take, and he advised following what the heart feels (rather than what the head thinks). The need to lead a disciplined life in order to have the clarity to choose is very similar to the effort needed to follow the *tao.*

Don Juan gave Castaneda the test question to be asked in choosing a path:*"Does this path have a heart?"* He went on to point out, that *"All paths are the same: They lead nowhere. They are paths going through the bush or into the bush."* (Traveling on the path with heart is the point; destination is immaterial. Don Juan seems to be describing an inner path like the **tao,** and to be emphasizing process rather than goal). He then contrasted the consequence of making a choice:

> Does this path have heart? If it does, the path is good; if it doesn't, it is of no use. Both paths lead nowhere; but one has a heart, the other doesn't. One makes for a joyful journey; as long as you follow it, you are one with it. The other will make you curse your life. One makes you strong; the other weakens you.

To know how to choose a path with heart is to learn how to follow the inner beat of *intuitive feeling.* Logic can tell you superficially where a path may lead to, but it cannot judge whether your heart will be in it. It is worthwhile to scan every life choice with rational thinking, but wrong to base a life choice on it. Choosing whom to marry or what to do as a life work, or what principles to base one's life on require that one's heart be in the choice. Rational thinking may be an excellent attendant or helper, but it cannot know or feel what is intangibly valuable and what ultimately gives meaning.

Don Juan warns of the necessity, in choosing a path, to be free of fear or ambition and counsels looking at every path closely and deliberately. The *Tao Te Ching* also speaks of the possibility of becoming confused or numbed by the variety of superficial attributes:

> The five colors blind the eye.
> The five tones deafen the ear.
> The five flavors dull the taste.
> Racing and hunting madden the mind.
> Precious things lead one astray.
> Therefore *the sage is guided by what he feels*

and not what he sees.
He lets go of that and chooses this.

In making life choices, ambition or fear are clearly strong forces that can influence or decide which path to take. Don Juan's warning is well taken, however, for both do result in unfulfilling journeys. If one is motivated by ambition, seeking either power or prestige, one is always concerned about how one is doing relative to others. Such a path is a race course in which one overtakes others and in turn fears that a similar fate is in store. When people are motivated by fear, they choose a path because it seems relatively safe. They select a career for financial security, choose a spouse as a good match who conforms to what is expected. They hope to avoid criticism by not risking "making a mistake." When fear or ambition are decisive, the heart is not even consulted. And eventually, as Don Juan warns, such a path will make you curse your life.

The *I Ching* also speaks of the need to make choices from the heart, to be true to oneself under all conditions. It says, *"If one is sincere when confronted with difficulties, the heart can penetrate the meaning of the situation, and once we have gained inner mastery of the problem, it will come about naturally that the action we take will succeed"* (from Hexagram 29, "The Abysmal").

Deliberation, thoughtfulness, and consciousness while traveling along a path means pausing between events or situations to consider and choose what to do, which way to go. If consciousness intervenes between stimulus and response, we can make conscious choices rather than following instinctive or programmed responses. Each choice finds us at a crossroad considering which path has heart and which might be muddled by ambition or fear and should be avoided.

In *Courage to Create,* Rollo May speaks of the potential we have for creating ourselves by our choices and by our commitment to them:

In human beings, courage is necessary to make being and becoming possible. An assertion of self, a commitment, is essential if the self is to have any reality. This is the distinction between human beings and the rest of nature. The acorn becomes an oak by means of automatic growth; no commitment is necessary. The kitten similarly becomes a cat on the basis of instinct. *Nature* and *Being* are identical in creatures like them. But a man or a woman becomes fully human only by his or her choices and his or her commitment to them. People attain worth and dignity by the multitude of decisions they make from day to day.

Psychologically, choosing a path with heart, achieving a sense of wholeness, making choices that lead to greater consciousness, and becoming fully human all have to do with being in touch with the archetype of the Self. Then our actions come from flowing with the Tao—our choices then are based on love and on faith that love is the best inner compass.

In one form or other, practically everyone at one time or another has experienced the Self, intuitively knowing that love and wisdom exist. Most often it has happened in one's youth, when a person is much more open and trusting. But the Self is experienced from time to time throughout life. The problem is not to "find it" some day. The difficulty is in maintaining an awareness of the Self once it has been experienced.

Herman Hesse's book *Journey to the East* is about a man who once traveled with a group of others, referred to as the League, on a unique and wonderful journey: *"Our goal was not only to the East, or rather the East was not only a country and something geographical, but it was the home and youth of the soul, it was everywhere and nowhere, it was the union of all times."* The pilgrimage to the East was both the narrator's particular adventure and a movement throughout history of believers and disciples, a stream of human beings, following the *"eternal strivings of the human spirit, toward the East, toward Home."* The narrator then lost touch with his companions and left the pilgrimage. Living an empty and meaningless life, he had lost his way and assumed that the League no longer existed because he no longer knew of it—

when in actuality it had continued and would for all time. The *Journey to the East,* which may be autobiographical, is a personal analogy for a great many people who once trusted intuitive feeling, knew that a path with heart existed, were in touch with the underlying Tao, and then, in their later cynicism and rationalism, proclaimed that "God is dead"—when what was dead was the spirit within them.

But finding the "League" again once it is lost, returning to the path with heart, or regaining access to the collective unconscious and the archetype of the Self is possible, when it is valued and sought. The way back is by several routes. One way is to remember what was once previously experienced, to dwell for a while on it, holding on to the details and memory. This way is a form of meditation. Then the experience of the Tao, or the Self, or of God—however it personally is conceptualized—can be returned to repeatedly as an inner experience. It may not be as moving or as profound as the original spontaneous mystical event itself, but recall carries feeling and inner warmth and reminds us of our spiritual values. Meditation, recalling the memory of a mystical experience, or prayer are themselves nourishing psychologically, providing a means to renew and reaffirm something of great inner value.

We can also seek reconnection with and renewal of the Tao experience by returning to the places or situations where it may likely happen. For some people, visiting a cathedral or chapel to pray may provide access. Others may need to set aside time to go into nature—climbing mountains, backpacking in the wilderness, strolling along the beach, or sitting in the woods. Still another access is through solitary creative activity, painting, writing poetry, or playing the flute help some people to reconnect to a spiritual source. Listening to music is another way; some music reaches deeply within and "re-souls" us.

All these ways require us to take *time* from the relentless treadmill schedule of activities that so often fill up our lives and leave us inwardly empty. Following the inner tao path requires us to stop for reflection and spiritual renewal as we journey through life. Spiritual renewal, emotional nourishment, access to an inner source, a sense of being one with nature, or in touch with the Tao occur during periods in which our experience of time alters from our usual clock-watching mentality. We have only one word for time; the Greeks had two, each one describing a difference in the experience and quality of time. One was *kronos,* time as we usually "watch it," measured time passing. It is our scheduled life, when we must get to work, when our appointments are, time we must account for, Father Time. The second, *kairos,* was very different. Rather than *measured* time, it is *participation* in time; time that so engrosses us that we lose track of time; timeless time; moments when the clock stands still; nourishing, renewing, more maternal time. Kairos time occurs on vacations when we are relaxed and lolling in the sun and when time seems to have accommodated to our needs and stretched out. It happens when we are completely involved in what we are doing. It always accompanies moments of emotional meaning or spiritual significance—time when we feel "one with," rather than separate from, the Self, the Tao, the love that connects us to others.

Opportunities to get back in touch with inner priorities, to reexperience a moment of timelessness in time, exist as invitations to return. Dreams and synchronistic events send repeated messages for us to receive. Like the Christian metaphor about the shepherd seeking his lost sheep, the cut-off, intuitive, feeling, spiritual inner aspect of the psyche keeps seeking reconciliation. The inner path beckons; the decision to follow it is up to us.

Paying attention to dreams and synchronistic events is another way of getting our bearings. Whether attended to or not, dreams and synchronistic events go on happening; if one does not decide to pay attention and attempt to remember, they slip by unnoticed. As the Talmud states, *"An unexamined dream is like an unopened letter."* Each dream or synchronistic event is an invitation to look inward.

If a person is traveling along a path that goes against his or her inner values and feelings, and in the process is changing for the worse, chances are that the dreams will be negative, often filled with unpleasant or hostile figures, which are *not* being confronted. "Negative" synchronicity carries a similar message to reflect on what one is doing. "Negative synchronicity" describes the piling up of coincidental events that block, hinder, and frustrate what one is attempting.

Conversely, when a person is following a path with heart, his or her dreams are usually nourishing; they seem interesting and pleasant, often imparting a sense of well-being. Synchronistically, opportunities seem to open fortuitously, the people we should meet accidentally cross our path, a flow or ease accompanies our work. Each facilitating, unsought event then begins to confer a feeling of being blessed, each serving as a lantern along the way, illuminating the path with heart.

To travel this path with heart, a person has an inner world in which the ego is filled with a spiritual abundance from its connection with the Self. There is generosity and freedom from fear within the psyche and in the world. Synchronistically, people cross our path and events unfold, facilitating rather than hindering the course we are on. The sense of fullness and flow influences the sense of time; there seems to be enough time to do whatever we are here for; even parking places synchronistically materialize.

If we are inwardly in "a really good place," we seem to be "humming along"—a common, fitting description for this state. It is interesting that the word "humming" is vibrationally like "om-ing," as in the Sanskrit *"Om mani padme hum,"* which is possibly the most widely used mantra in the Eastern world. (A mantra is a sound or phrase repeated over and over again, and designed to get a person into a certain harmony with the universe.) So when we "hum along," it is as if we are aware of being connected with the underlying pattern of oneness in the universe. It is as if we are part of the cosmic dance around the still point, hearing the faint hum of the music as we move—in tune with the Tao.

CHAPTER 9

THE MESSAGE OF THE TAO EXPERIENCE: WE ARE NOT ALONE

The Tao experience · The profound awareness of being part of something far greater than ourselves · The Kingdom of God · The rainmaker and returning to the Tao · The Grail Legend · Tao as connection between us and the universe

Almost everyone, at some time in his or her life, has had a Tao experience. It may have occurred on a mountain top, perceived as a wondrous sense of being one with the universe. It may have happened early one morning in a kitchen, as the room and the heart infused with an indescribable warmth and radiant light. Or it may have taken place on a lonely stretch of beach, after finding a fish vertebra shaped exactly like a butterfly—a symbolic gift from the sea that came at a time when the butterfly image was already charged with personal meaning from dreams and contemplation, received as a synchronistic event and instantly followed by an inward flooding of joy and love.

The Tao experience conveys a profound awareness of being part of something far greater than ourselves, of being included, loved, and in touch with an invisible, eternal reality. In that timeless moment, when the Tao is experienced, we know that this is more significant than the tangible world around us and far more meaningful than our usual, everyday concerns. At that moment, everything and everyone seem synchronistically connected, linked by an underlying spiritual meaning.

What is known intuitively, through experience of the Tao, is that we are not lonely, isolated, insignificant, and meaningless creatures, accidentally evolved from organic rubbish on a miniscule dot in the vast cosmos. Instead, the Tao experience gives us the direct knowledge that we are linked to all others and to the universe, through that which underlies everything and which some call God. Synchronistic events are glimpses into this underlying oneness, which is the meaning conveyed through an uncanny coincidence. The unseen linkage is moves us; the synchronistic event tells us we are not alone.

At the end of a lecture I once gave on synchronicity, a man in the audience came up to talk with me, to share an event of synchronicity through which he felt this kind of connection. It was during World War II; he was then a young black fighter pilot, temporarily training on a segregated Air Force base in the Deep South. It was Christmas time, and he was lonely and isolated, missing the warmth and festivity of his family celebrations in Southern California. For the first time in his life, he experienced the intense racial animosity directed toward black servicemen when they went into town; it made him virtually a prisoner, confined to base. One evening he was walking around, feeling more miserable and lonely than he ever had in his life, when he heard singing in the chapel—a Christmas choir was rehearsing. Entering the chapel, he sat in a back row and listened to the familiar carols. Then he started thinking of his grandfather, a powerful, loving, protective man, a Baptist head deacon who loved to sing and who had often taken his reluctant grandson to church with him. The hymn his grandfather had loved best —not a Christmas carol—came flooding into his mind: "I Come to the Garden Alone."

This man said to me, "I was missing him terribly and thinking that I would really like to hear this song, and then for some reason I felt a presence and a certainty. I *knew* that the choir was going to sing it—and it seemed that in the very next moment they began, '*I come to the garden alone, while the dew is still on the flowers, and He walks with me, and He talks with me, and He tells me I am His own.*'" Tears came welling up, as I felt a tremendous joy, the most peaceful state in my life." The synchronistic event brought him an immediate sense of being cared for and no longer isolated. He experienced that oneness that is so difficult to put into words and yet is so absolutely convincing.

An uncanny, meaningful coincidence seems to lead to an awareness of an underlying connecting principle, as synchronistic events evoke an intuitively felt spiritual reality. Conversely, becoming spiritually centered, in touch with the Tao, is associated with the occurrence of positive synchronistic events. Being in touch with the Tao seems to prompt an easy flow of outer events *through* synchronicity. This is the message of religious teachings in both East and West: Seek spiritual values first; whatever is tangibly needed will follow after.

In his ministry, Jesus preached about the Kingdom of God, exhorting people to seek this highest value, saying it was at hand and possible to attain. This Kingdom of God has been interpreted metaphorically to mean the possibility of a direct experience of a loving, eternal God. In Jesus' teachings about "the birds of the air" and of "the lilies of the field," it seems to me that he is saying that synchronicity will provide for material needs if first one seeks the Kingdom of God:

Look at the birds of the air: they neither sow nor reap nor gather into barns, and yet your heavenly Father feeds them. Are you not of more value than they? And which of you by being anxious can add one cubit to his span of life? And why are you anxious about clothing? Consider the lilies of the field, how they grow; they neither toil nor spin, yet I tell you, even Solomon in all his glory was not arrayed like one of these. But if God so clothes the grass of the field, which today is alive and tomorrow is thrown into the oven, will he not much more clothe you, O men of little faith? Therefore do not be anxious, saying, 'What shall we eat? or 'What shall we drink?' or 'What shall we wear' . . . your heavenly Father knows you need them all. *But seek first his Kingdom and his righteousness, and all these things shall be yours as well.* Matthew 6:26–30

To the Eastern mind, "returning to the Tao" carries a meaning similar to "finding the Kingdom of God." Richard Wilhelm, who had lived in China, told Jung the story of the rainmaker of Kiaochau: a story which is a marvelous psychological parable about synchronicity and its relationship to the Tao.

There was a great drought. For months there had not been a drop of rain and the situation became catastrophic. The Catholics made processions, the Protestants made prayers and the Chinese burned joss-sticks and shot off guns to frighten away the demons of the drought, but with no result. Finally the Chinese said, "We will fetch the rainmaker." And from another province a dried-up old man appeared. The only thing he asked for was a quiet little house somewhere, and there he locked himself in for three days. On the fourth day the clouds gathered and there was a great snow storm at the time of the year when no snow was expected, an unusual amount, and the town was so full of rumors about the wonderful rainmaker that Richard Wilhelm went to ask the man how he did it. In true European fashion he said, "They call you the rainmaker, will you tell me how you made the snow?" And the little Chineseman said, "I did not make the snow, I am not responsible." "But what have you done these three days?" "Oh, I can explain that. I come from another country where things are in order. Here they are out of order, they are not as they should be by the ordinance of heaven. Therefore the whole country is not in Tao, and I also am not in the natural order of things because I am in a disordered country. So I had to wait three days *until I was back in Tao and then naturally the rain came.*" C. G. Jung, *Mysterium Coniunctionis*, pp. 419–420

The rainmaker described the drought-afflicted country to which he had traveled as being a *disordered country* and attributed the drought and suffering to not being in Tao. To me, "living in a disordered country" means psychologically that the ego experiences itself in a state where there is a lack of underlying order. In such a situation, there is anxiety and fear of emotional or material scarcity. The feeling that there is not enough to go around now and fear that there will be even less in the future is the "drought mentality," which then follows. Then everyone else becomes a potential competitor in a lawless psychological jungle, full of predators, each "looking out for number 1."

On arriving in this disordered country, the rainmaker withdrew to his quiet little house, locked himself in it for three days, waiting until he "was back in Tao and then naturally the rain came." To be back in Tao psychologically is to again experience being part of the oneness that underlies and nourishes all things, to connect again with what Jung calls the Self, to feel the abundance of love which is available both to give and to receive. Being back in Tao is another way of saying, "I feel centered again, in touch with a sense that life has meaning." Being back in Tao means that "I can live optimistically, trusting that there will be enough of whatever is needed." "And then naturally the rain came" is the promise of the rainmaker principle of synchronicity. If the inner world is reflected in the outer world through synchronicity, then returning to the Tao inwardly of course resulted in a return of the rain, as a restoration of the natural order.

The parable of the rainmaker shares a symbolic similarity with the Grail Legend. Once again, there is a desolated country, a wasteland, where cattle do not reproduce, crops won't grow, knights are killed, children are orphaned, maidens weep, and there is mourning everywhere. This time the country's problems are related to the wounded Fisher King, who suffers continuously because his wound will not heal.

The Grail is in his castle, but the King cannot touch or be healed by it until, as prophesied, an innocent young man comes to the court and asks the question, "Whom does the Grail serve?" The Grail was the legendary communion cup used by Jesus at the Last Supper and is a symbol of Christ or the Self (Christ and Self both describe something beyond human or ego, something that is divine, spiritual, reconciling, and gives meaning).

If the ruler of the country, the ego, could be touched by the Grail and experience the spirituality of the Self or inner Christ, it would have the power to heal him. Synchronistically, when his wound was healed the country would recover. Joy and growth would return. The wound may symbolize the situation of ego being cut off from the Self, where the separation is a wound that never heals and causes continuous pain in the form of persistent, chronic anxiety and depression.

The Fisher King's wound is the psychological problem of modern times. In a competitive, materialistic society, where cynicism toward spiritual values exists, where God has been declared dead, and neither scientific nor psychological thinking given any importance to the realm of the spirit, individuals feel isolated and insignificant. Seeking sexual intimacy to cure isolation or seeking assertiveness as a solution to feeling insignificant does not heal the wound. When the ego is cut off from experiencing the Self—or, put differently, when an individual lacks the inner sense of being connected to God or being part of the Tao—then a wound exists that the person experiences as gnawing, pervasive, persisting insecurity. All kinds of defensive maneuvers, from smoking to amassing power, are unsatisfying efforts to feel better. The narcissism of modern times seems fueled by the feeling of being deprived and unnourished emotionally or spiritually, which is part of the same wound. A person thus wounded seeks novelty, excitement, power, or prestige to compensate for a lack of joy or inner peace. Chronic anger and depression seem to hide just below the surface of the persona, or face presented to the world. Again, this is a consequence of the wound, of the ego being cut off from the Self. This wound affects the capacity to both give and receive love. Emotionally, scarcity rather than abundance prevails, and thus generosity, compassion, giving hope and helping all are constricted, and joy and growth are stifled.

T. S. Eliot is describing the emotional desolation and barrenness of the Fisher King's realm in his poem *"The Wasteland,"* which has the Grail Legend as one of its major themes. This poem describes a spiritually barren country where one lives in a state of perpetual drought, experiencing life as dry—meaningless and loveless—waiting for the rain that never comes and unable to escape from the all-pervasive emotional isolation and meaningless activity.

To restore life to the wasteland, the Fisher King's wound must be healed. The king can be equated with the ruling psychological principle of the psyche—that which the ego uses to determine value and make choices. For many individuals, and certainly for our culture as a whole—rationalism or scientific thinking is the ruling principle. In the Grail Legend, it is cut off from the spiritual communion vessel, through which healing and return of vitality would flow. The wound that will not heal is a result of the severing of a connection crucial to well-being. The King cut off from the Grail is the rationalist ego cut off from spirituality, thinking separated from intuitive feeling, the "type A" heart attack-prone, linear personality cut off from everything that is nonrational and gives meaning.

The King cannot touch or be healed by the Grail until an innocent young man—sometimes described as an innocent young "fool," enters the scene. From the standpoint of the "ruling" principle, which here is rational thinking, the wound will stay continuously open and unhealed until a new element enters the psychological situation. It may be that only the young, naive, innocent element within the psyche —which from the perspective of worldly thinking would be considered the fool—can experience the wonder and awe of the Grail, a Christ symbol, and can ask questions about meaning, which then can lead to a restoration of a connection between the ego and the Self. Then the internal landscape, which has been a wasteland or dry desert, may bloom and be green again, as emotion and spiritual feeling, the irrational elements in touch with the symbolic layer of the unconscious, are brought into the personality.

In considering how all of the many parables, metaphors, spiritual teachings, and psychological insights noted in this book might fit together, I have the following impressionistic, subjective conception. It seems to me that the Christian vision of the Kingdom of God, the Eastern vision of the Tao, Jung's idea of the Self and synchronicity, the right hemisphere's intuitive way of perceiving totality and containing opposites, the parapsychological evidence for consciousness separate from brain or body, and the new reality as seen by quantum physics are all part of the same ineffable, invisible, meaning-giving "something." Each is a glimpse from a different vantage point—each gives us a different impression that is true but not complete. Like the six blind men who groped for the reality of the elephant, we can grasp only part at a time. In this tale from India, the first blind man fell against the elephant's side and said the elephant was like a wall. The second felt the tip of the tusk and was convinced an elephant was like a spear. The third, on feeling the squirming trunk, proclaimed an elephant was like a snake. The fourth put his arms around a leg and said an elephant was like a tree. The fifth, who felt the ear, declared an elephant was very much a fan; while the sixth, on seizing the tail, said of course an elephant was like a rope. All then fell to arguing about who had the truth. While each of them had part of the picture, all of them missed the whole.

Or perhaps we are like Plato's chained men in the cave, unable to see out, seeing only the fleeting shadows cast against the wall, making up theories and certainties about what is outside the cave. We can never fully grasp what is boundless, infinite, and eternal. Yet that small insight glimpsed or intuition felt—of the reality of the Tao, or of God, or the Self, in whatever form—is psychologically central to human experience. It nourishes our spirit, heals our sense of isolated separateness, and restores our soul.

In an episode of "Star Trek," a being from another world, whose form was that of conscious energy unbound in matter, needed to be at the controls of the starship *Enterprise*. For this, he needed to borrow a body, and so with Spock's permission, he entered Spock's body, trying it on as one would a suit of clothes. His first words of surprise and pain were "How lonely it is!" as he experienced the separateness that is also part of the human experience. The deeper significance of synchronicity lies in its demonstration of certain aspects of the collective unconscious, which behaves as if it were one and were not split up into many individuals, animals, and the environment. In the synchronistic moment, the separate "I" no longer feels "How lonely it is"; instead, the person directly experiences a sense of oneness. This is what is so deeply moving in experiences of synchronicity and is why these events are often felt as numinous, religious, or spiritual experiences. When we feel synchronicity, we feel ourselves as part of a cosmic matrix, as participants in the Tao. It gives us a glimpse into the reality that there is indeed a link between us all, between us and all living things, between us and the universe.

References

All references to Jung's *Collected Works* are taken from *Collected Works of C. G. Jung,* eds. Sir Herbert Read, Michael Fordham and Gerhard Adler, trans. by R. F. C. Hull, Bollingen series XX, published by Princeton University Press, New Jersey. Executive editor is William McGuire.

Chapter 1: What the Tao Is—What the Dance Is

Adam, Michael. *Wandering in Eden: Three Ways to the East Within Us.* New York: Knopf, 1976.

Blyth, R. H. *Haiku.* Vol. 1: *Eastern Culture.* Japan: Hokuseido, 1949, p. 198.

Capra, Fritjof. *The Tao of Physics.* Boulder, Colo.: Shambala, 1976; New York: Bantam Books, 1977.

Eliot, T. S. *Four Quartets: Burnt Norton.* New York: Harcourt Brace Jovanovich, 1943.

Franck, Frederick. *The Zen of Seeing: Seeing/Drawing as Meditation.* New York: Random House, 1973.

Galin, David. "Implications for Psychiatry of Left and Right Cerebral Specialization." *Archives of General Psychiatry* 31 (October 1974): 572–583.

Jung, C. G. "Foreword to *East Asia Thinks Otherwise* by Lily Abegg" in Jung's *Collected Works,* Vol. 18 (1976), p. 655.

Lao Tsu. *Tao Te Ching, One.* Translation by Gia-Fu Feng and Jane English. New York: Random House, 1972.

Sze, Mai-Mai. *The Tao of Painting.* Vol. 1. Bollingen Series 49. New York: Pantheon Books, 1956, Chap. 1: "On Tao and the Tao."

Chapter 2: Jung, Synchronicity, and the Self

Bolen, Jean Shinoda. "Synchronicity, Jung's View." In *International Encyclopedia of Psychiatry, Psychoanalysis and Neurology.* New York: Van Nostrand Reinhold, 1977. Vol II, pp. 67–70.

Frey-Wehrlin, C. T. "Reflection of C. G. Jung's Concept of Synchronicity." *Journal of Analytical Psychology,* 1976, *21* (1), 37–49.

The I Ching, or *Book of Changes.* Translation by Richard Wilhelm and Cary F. Baynes. Foreword by C. G. Jung. Bollingen Series 19. Princeton, N. J.: Princeton University Press, 1950.

Jung, C. G. "In Memoriam, For Richard Wilhelm." *Collected Works.* Vol. 15 (1930), pp. 53–62.

Jung, C. G. "On Synchronicity." *Collected Works.* Vol. 8 (1951), pp. 520–531.

Jung, C. G. "Synchronicity: An Acausal Connecting Principle." *Collected Works.* Vol. 8 (1952), pp. 417–519.

Jung, C. G. "Foreword," *I Ching*, or *Book of Changes.* Translated by Richard Wilhelm and Cary F. Baynes. Bollingen Series XIX. Princeton, N.J.: Princeton University Press, 1950, pp. xix-xxxix.

Jung, C. G. *Letters.* Selected and edited by G. Adler in collaboration with A. Jaffe. Vol. 1 (1906–1950), p. 395.

Jung, C. G. *Memories, Dreams and Reflections.* New York: Pantheon Books, 1961, chap. VI, "Confrontation with the Unconscious."

Jung, C. G. Foreword and Commentary to *The Secret of the Golden Flower: A Chinese Book of Life,* translated by Richard Wilhelm. New York: Harcourt Brace Jovanovich, 1931.

Jung, C. G. "The Archetypes and the Collective Unconscious." *Collected Works,* Vol. 9, Part I: "Archetypes of the Collective Unconscious" (1934) pp. 3–41; "The Concept of the Collective Unconscious" (1936) pp. 42–53; "Concerning Mandala Symbolism" (1950) pp. 355–384.

Chapter 3: The Agatha Christie Approach to Synchronicity

Dieckmann, Hans. "The Constellation of the Countertransference in Relation to the Presentation of Archetypal Dreams: Research Methods and Results." In Gerhard Adler, ed., *Success and Failure in Analysis.* New York: Putman's, 1974. (This article contains information on ESP and Synchronicity in analysis.)

Jung, C. G. *Memories, Dreams and Reflections.* New York: Pantheon Books, 1961, p. 137.

Spiegelberg, Frederic. Lecture, "Reflections on Sanskrit Terms—A Psychological Guide to Eastern Wisdom," October 28, 1978, at C. G. Jung Institute, San Francisco.

Chapter 4: Significant Meetings and the Synchronistic Matchmaker

Bach, Richard. *Illusions: The Adventures of a Reluctant Messiah.* New York: Delacorte Press/Eleanor Friede, 1977, p. 110.

Jung, C. G. "Problems of Modern Psychotherapy." *Collected Works,* Vol. 16 (1966), p. 71.

Chapter 5: Like a Waking Dream

Dement, William C. "Sleep and Dreams." In A. M. Freedman and H. I. Kaplan, eds., *Comprehensive Textbook of Psychiatry.* Baltimore: Williams & Wilkins, 1967.

Chapter 6: Synchronistic Wisdom of the I Ching

Henderson, Joseph L. "A Commentary on the *Book of Changes*, the *I Ching*." *Psychic* 3, no. 2 (September-October 1971): pp. 9–12, 46.

Holy Bible. Revised Standard Version. New York: Nelson, 1973, Ecclesiastes 3:1–2.

The *I Ching*, or *Book of Changes*. Translated by Richard Wilhelm and Cary F. Baynes. Bollingen Series XIX. Princeton, N. J.: Princeton University Press, 1950.

Jung, C. G. "Foreword to the *I Ching*, Wilhelm-Baynes translation." Bollingen Series XIX. Princeton, N. J.: Princeton University Press, 1950.

Chapter 7: Parapsychological Pieces of the Synchronicity Puzzle

Bolen, Jean Shinoda. "Interview—Dr. J. B. Rhine." *Psychic* 3, no. 6 (July 1972): 7–10, 30–34.

Eliot, T. S. *The Four Quartets: Dry Salvages.* New York: Harcourt Brace Jovanovich, 1943.

Jung, C. G. *Memories, Dreams and Reflections.* New York: Pantheon Books, 1961.

Koestler, Arthur. *The Roots of Coincidence.* New York: Random House, 1973.

Lilly, John C. *The Center of the Cyclone: An Autobiography of Inner Space.* New York: Julian Press, 1972.

"Interview, Uri Geller," *Psychic* 4, no. 5 (May-June 1975): 6–10, 30–32.

Progoff, Ira. *Jung, Synchronicity and Human Destiny.* New York: Dell, 1973, pp. 104–106. Reprinted by arrangement with the Julian Press, copyright 1973 by Ira Progoff.

Schneidler, Gertrude, ed. *Extrasensory Perception.* New York: Atherton, 1969. (A collection of "milestone" parapsychological papers, including her "sheep" and "goat" experiment.)

Vaughan, Alan. "Interview, Gertrude Schneidler." *Psychic* 3, no. 4 (January-February, 1972): 4–6, 32–36.

Vaughan, Alan. "Poltergeist Investigations in Germany." *Psychic* 1, no. 5 (March-April, 1970): 9–13.

Vaughan, Alan. "The Phenomenon of Uri Geller." *Psychic* 4, no. 5 (May-June, 1973): 13–18.

Chapter 8: The Tao as Path with Heart

Castaneda, Carlos. *The Teachings of Don Juan: A Yaqui Way of Knowledge.* New York: Simon & Schuster, 1974, p. 107. (Originally published 1968.)

Hesse, Hermann. *Journey to the East.* Translated by Hilda Rosner. New York: Farrar, Straus & Giroux, 1961.

The *I Ching*, or *Book of Changes*. Translated by Richard Wilhelm and Cary F. Baynes. Bollingen Series XIX. Princeton, N. J.: Princeton University Press, 1950.

Lao Tsu. *Tao Te Ching, Twelve.* Translated by Gia-Fu Feng and Jane English. New York: Random House, 1972.

May, Rollo. *Courage to Create.* New York: Norton, 1975, pp. 13-14.

Sze, Mai-Mai. "On Tao and the Tao" in *The Tao of Painting.* Vol. 1. Bollingen Series 49. New York: Pantheon Books, 1956.

Chapter 9: The Message of the Tao Experience: We Are Not Alone

Eliot, T. S. *The Wasteland.* Edited and with an introduction by Valerie Eliot. New York: Harcourt Brace Jovanovich, 1971. (A facsimile and transcript of the original drafts, including the annotations of Ezra Pound.)

Johnson, Robert A. *He: Understanding Male Psychology.* New York: Harper & Row, 1977. (Discusses the meaning of the Grail Legend.)

Jung, C. G. "Mysterium Coiunctionis." *Collected Works.* Vol. 14 (1963), pp. 419–420, footnote.

Holy Bible, Revised Standard Version. New York: Nelson, 1953.

Index